THE COMPLETE GREEK TRAGEDIES

VOLUME III

SOPHOCLES I

OEDIPUS THE KING

OEDIPUS AT COLONUS

ANTIGONE

Edited by DAVID GRENE and RICHMOND LATTIMORE

THE MODERN LIBRARY · NEW YORK

Random House IS THE PUBLISHER OF *The Modern Library*
BENNETT CERF · DONALD S. KLOPFER
Manufactured in the United States of America

CONTENTS

THE COMPLETE GREEK TRAGEDIES

VOLUME III

SOPHOCLES I

OEDIPUS THE KING

OEDIPUS AT COLONUS

ANTIGONE

INTRODUCTION

"The Theban Plays" by Sophocles

This series of plays, *Oedipus the King, Oedipus at Colonus,* and *Antigone,* was written over a wide interval of years. The dating is only approximate, for reliable evidence is lacking; but the *Antigone* was produced in 441 B.C. when Sophocles was probably fifty-four, and *Oedipus the King* some fourteen or fifteen years later. *Oedipus at Colonus* was apparently produced the year after its author's death at the age of ninety in 405 B.C. Thus, although the three plays are concerned with the same legend, they were not conceived and executed at the same time and with a single purpose, as is the case with Aeschylus' *Oresteia.* We can here see how a story teased the imagination of Sophocles until it found its final expression. We can see the degrees of variation in treatment he gave the myth each time he handled it. And perhaps we can come to some notion of what the myths meant to Sophocles as raw material for the theater.

The internal dramatic dates of the three plays do not agree with the order of their composition. As far as the legend is concerned, the story runs in sequence: *Oedipus the King, Oedipus at Colonus, Antigone.* But Sophocles wrote them in the order: *Antigone, Oedipus the King, Oedipus at Colonus.* In view of this and the long interval between the composition of the individual plays, we would expect some inconsistencies between the three versions. And there are fairly serious inconsistencies—in facts, for instance. At the conclusion of *Oedipus the King,* Creon is in undisputed authority after the removal

3

of Oedipus. Though he appeals to him to look after his daughters, Oedipus refrains from asking Creon to do anything for his sons, who, he says, will be all right on their own (*OK* 1460). It is Creon who will succeed Oedipus in Thebes, and there is no question of any legitimate claim of Oedipus' descendants (*OK* 1418). But in *Antigone*, Creon tells the chorus that he has favorably observed their loyalty first to Oedipus and then to his sons, and so has hope of their devotion to himself. In *Oedipus at Colonus*—the last of the three plays he wrote— Sophocles makes one of his very few clumsy efforts to patch the discrepancies together. In *Oedipus at Colonus* (ll. 367 ff.), Ismene says that *at first* the two sons were willing to leave the throne to Creon in view of their fatal family heritage, but after a while they decided to take over the monarchy and the quarrel was only between themselves as to who should succeed. At this point Creon has vanished out of the picture altogether! Again, the responsibility for the decision to expel Oedipus from Thebes and keep him out rests, in *Oedipus the King*, entirely with Creon, who announces that he will consult Apollo in the matter. In *Oedipus at Colonus* his sons' guilt in condemning their father to exile is one of the bitterest counts in Oedipus' indictment of them (*OC* 1360 ff.). These are important differences. We do not know anything really certain about the manner of publication of the plays after their production. We know even less about Sophocles' treatment of his own scripts. Maybe he simply did not bother to keep them after he saw them as far as the stage, though that seems unlikely. Or it is possible and likelier that Sophocles, as he wrote the last play in extreme old age and in what seems to be the characteristic self-absorption of the last years of his life, cared little about whether *Oedipus at Colonus* exactly tallied, in its presentation, with the stories he had written thirty-seven and twenty-two years earlier.

Let us for the moment disregard the details of the story and concentrate on what would seem to be the central theme of the first two plays in order of composition. And here we find something very curious. Most critics have felt the significance of the *Antigone* to lie in the opposition of Creon and Antigone and all that this opposition represents. It is thus a play about something quite different from *Oedipus the King*. And yet what a remarkable similarity there is in the dilemma of Creon in *Antigone* and Oedipus himself in the first Oedipus play. In both of them a king has taken a decision which is disobeyed or questioned by his subjects. In both, the ruler misconstrues the role of the rebel and his own as a sovereign. In both, he has a crucial encounter with the priest Teiresias, who warns him that the forces of religion are against him. In both, he charges that the priest has been suborned. There the resemblance ends; for, after abusing the old prophet, Creon is overcome with fear of his authority and, too late, tries to undo his mistake. In *Oedipus the King* the king defies all assaults upon his decision until the deadly self-knowledge which starts to work in him has accomplished its course and he is convicted out of his own mouth.

Usually, as we know, the *Antigone* is interpreted entirely as the conflict between Creon and Antigone. It has often been regarded as the classical statement of the struggle between the law of the individual conscience and the central power of the state. Unquestionably, these issues are inherent in the play. Unquestionably, even, Sophocles would understand the modern way of seeing his play, for the issue of the opposition of the individual and the state was sufficiently present to his mind to make this significant for him. But can the parallelism between the position of Oedipus in the one play and Creon in the other be quite irrelevant to the interpretation of the two? And is it not very striking that such a large share of the *Antigone* should be devoted to the conclusion of the conflict, as far as Creon is concerned, and to the destruction of his human happiness?

What I would suggest is this: that Sophocles had at the time of writing the first play (in 442 B.C.) a theme in mind which centered in the Theban trilogy. One might express it by saying that it is the story of a ruler who makes a mistaken decision, though in good faith, and who then finds himself opposed in a fashion which he misunderstands and which induces him to persist in his mistake. This story is later on going to be that of a man who breaks divine law without realizing that he is doing so, and whose destruction is then brought about by the voice of the divine law in society. Between the *Antigone* and *Oedipus the King*, the theme has developed further, for in the latter play Sophocles is showing how the ruler who breaks the divine law may, for all he can see and understand, be entirely innocent, but nonetheless his guilt is an objective fact. In the third play, *Oedipus at Colonus*, this issue reaches its final statement. The old Oedipus is admittedly a kind of monster. Wherever he comes, people shrink from him. Yet his guilt carries with it some sort of innocence on which God will set his seal. For the old man is both cursed and blessed. The god gives him an extraordinary end, and the last place of his mortal habitation is blessed forever.

What this interpretation would mean, if correct, is that Sophocles started to write about the Theban legend, the story of Oedipus and his children, without having fully understood what he wanted to say about it. He may have been, and probably was, drawn, unknown to himself, to the dramatization of this particular legend because in it lay the material of the greatest theme of his later artistic life. But first he tried his hand at it in the opposition of Creon and Antigone. However, even while he did this, the character of Creon and his role in the play were shaping what was to be the decisive turn in the story he was going to write—the Oedipus saga.

Thus there is a certain elasticity in the entire treatment of myth. The author will accent a certain character at one time to suit a play and change the accent to suit another. Or he may even discover the same theme in a different myth. This is suggested by a short comparison of the *Philoctetes* and *Oedipus at Colonus*, both written in the last few years of Sophocles' life. The figure of Philoctetes, though occurring in a totally

6

different legend from Oedipus, is a twin child with Oedipus in Sophocles' dramatic imagination. In both these plays, the *Philoctetes* and *Oedipus at Colonus*, the hero is a man whose value is inextricably coupled with his offensive quality. Philoctetes is the archer whose bow will overcome Troy. He is also the creature whose stinking infested wound moves everyone to disgust who has to do with him. Oedipus is accursed in the sight of all men; he had committed the two crimes, parricide and incest, which rendered him an outcast in any human society. But he is also the one to whom, at his end, God will give the marks of his favor, and the place where he is last seen on earth will be lucky and blessed. This combination of the evil and the good is too marked, in these two plays, to be accidental. It is surely the idea which inspired the old Sophocles for his two last plays. There is, however, an important further development of the theme in the *Oedipus at Colonus*. For there in Oedipus' mind the rational innocence—the fact that he had committed the offenses unknowingly—is, for him at least, important in God's final justification of him. Sophocles is declaring that the sin of Oedipus is real; that the consequences in the form of the loneliness, neglect, and suffering of the years of wandering are inevitable; but that the will and the consciousness are also some measure of man's sin—and when the sinner sinned necessarily and unwittingly, his suffering can be compensation enough for his guilt. He may at the end be blessed and a blessing. This is not the same doctrine as that of Aeschylus, when he asserts that through suffering comes wisdom. Nor is it the Christian doctrine of a man purified by suffering as by fire. Oedipus in his contact with Creon, in his interview with Polyneices shows himself as bitter, sudden in anger, and implacable as ever. He is indeed a monstrous old man. But at the last, he is, in a measure, *vindicated*. Yet in *Philoctetes* the theme of the union of the offensive and the beneficial, which in *Oedipus at Colonus* becomes the curse and the blessing, is seen without the addition of conscious innocence and unconscious guilt. Can we say that Sophocles finally felt that the consciousness of innocence in Oedipus is the balancing factor in the story? That in this sense *Oedipus at Colonus* is the further step beyond *Philoctetes* in the clarification of the dramatic subject which occupied the very old author? Or that the consciousness of innocence when linked with objective guilt is only the human shield against the cruelty of the irrational—that Oedipus is meaningful in his combination of guilt and innocence as a manifestation of God and of destiny and that his explanation of his conscious innocence is only the poor human inadequate explanation? Everyone will answer this according to his own choice. But, clearly, the theme of Philoctetes and the theme of the old Oedipus are connected.

If an analysis such as this has importance, it is to show the relation of Sophocles to the raw material of his plays—the myth. It is to show the maturing of a theme in Sophocles' mind and his successive treatments of it in the same and different legends. In the Oedipus story it is a certain fundamental situation which becomes significant for Sophocles, and the characters are altered to suit the story. Creon in the first, Oedipus in the second, are examples of the same sort of dilemma, even though the dilemma of Creon in the *Antigone* is incidental to the main emphasis of the play, which is on Antigone. But the dilemma was to be much more fruitful for Sophocles as a writer and thinker than the plain issue between Antigone and Creon. The dilemma resolves itself in the last play at the end of Sophocles' life into the dramatic statement of a principle, of the union of the blessed and the cursed, of the just and the unjust, and sometimes (not always) of the consciously innocent and the unconsciously guilty. The fact that Sophocles could in two successive treatments of the play fifteen years apart switch the parts of Creon and Oedipus indicates that neither the moral color of the characters nor even their identity was absolutely fixed in his mind. The same conclusion is borne out by the great similarity between the *Philoctetes* and the *Oedipus at Colonus*. Sophocles in his last days was incessantly thinking of the man who is blessed and cursed. For the theater he became once the lame castaway Philoctetes, who yet, in virtue of his archery, is to be the conqueror of Troy; in the next play he is Oedipus, who sinned against the order of human society but is still to be the blessing of Athens and the patron saint of Colonus. It is the theme and not the man that matters. Consequently, it is the kernel of the legend, as he saw it for the moment, that is sacred for Sophocles, not the identification of all the characters in a certain relation to one another. True, he has treated the Oedipus story three times in his life, which means that the Oedipus story had a certain fascination for him—that somehow hidden in it he knew there was what he wanted to say. But he did not have to think of the whole story and the interdependence of its characters when he made his changes each time. One stage of the theme borne by the hero is given to a character in a totally different myth. The sequence is Creon, Oedipus, Philoctetes, Oedipus. It may seem absurd to link Creon, the obvious form of tyrant (as conceived by the Athenians), and Philoctetes. But it is the progression we should notice. The tyrant who with true and good intentions orders what is wrong, morally and religiously, is crudely represented in Creon; he is much more subtly represented in Oedipus himself in the next play. But the similarity of the situation and the nature of the opposition to him proves how generically the character is conceived. You can switch the labels, and Creon becomes Oedipus. But if the character is generic, the situation is deepening. We are beginning to understand *why* a certain sort of tyrant may be a tyrant and in a shadowy way how conscious and unconscious guilt are related. In the *Philoctetes* and *Oedipus at Colonus* the situation is being seen in its last stages. We are no longer concerned with how Philoctetes came to sin or how Oedipus is the author of his own ruin. But only how does it feel to be an object both of disgust and of fear to your fellows, while you yourself are simultaneously

9

aware of the injustice of your treatment and at last, in *Oedipus at Colonus,* of the objective proofs of God's favor.

For Sophocles the myth was the treatment of the generic aspect of human dilemmas. What he made of the myth in his plays was neither history nor the kind of dramatic creation represented by *Hamlet* or *Macbeth.* Not history, for in no sense is the uniqueness of the event or the uniqueness of the character important; not drama in the Shakespearean sense, because Sophocles' figures do not have, as Shakespeare's do, the timeless and complete reality in themselves. Behind the figure of Oedipus or Creon stands the tyrant of the legend; and behind the tyrant of the legend, the meaning of all despotic authority. Behind the old Oedipus is the beggar and wanderer of the legend, and behind him the mysterious human combination of opposites—opposites in meaning and in fact. And so the character may fluctuate or the names may vary. It is the theme, the generic side of tragedy, which is important; it is there that the emphasis of the play rests.

DAVID GRENE

University of Chicago

SOPHOCLES I

OEDIPUS THE KING

OEDIPUS AT COLONUS

ANTIGONE

OEDIPUS THE KING

Translated by

DAVID GRENE

CHARACTERS

Oedipus, King of Thebes
Jocasta, His Wife
Creon, His Brother-in-Law
Teiresias, an Old Blind Prophet
A Priest
First Messenger
Second Messenger
A Herdsman
A Chorus of Old Men of Thebes

OEDIPUS THE KING

SCENE: *In front of the palace of Oedipus at Thebes. To
the right of the stage near the altar stands the Priest
with a crowd of children. Oedipus emerges from the
central door.*

Oedipus
Children, young sons and daughters of old Cadmus,
why do you sit here with your suppliant crowns?
The town is heavy with a mingled burden
of sounds and smells, of groans and hymns and incense;   5
I did not think it fit that I should hear
of this from messengers but came myself,—
I Oedipus whom all men call the Great.

(*He turns to the Priest.*)
You're old and they are young; come, speak for them.
What do you fear or want, that you sit here   10
suppliant? Indeed I'm willing to give all
that you may need; I would be very hard
should I not pity suppliants like these.

Priest
O ruler of my country, Oedipus,
you see our company around the altar;   15
you see our ages; some of us, like these,
who cannot yet fly far, and some of us
heavy with age; these children are the chosen
among the young, and I the priest of Zeus.

15

Within the market place sit others crowned   20
with suppliant garlands, at the double shrine
of Pallas and the temple where Ismenus
gives oracles by fire. King, you yourself
have seen our city reeling like a wreck
already; it can scarcely lift its prow
out of the depths, out of the bloody surf.
A blight is on the fruitful plants of the earth,   25
A blight is on the cattle in the fields,
a blight is on our women that no children
are born to them; a God that carries fire,
a deadly pestilence, is on our town,
strikes us and spares not, and the house of Cadmus
is emptied of its people while black Death
grows rich in groaning and in lamentation.   30
We have not come as suppliants to this altar
because we thought of you as of a God,
but rather judging you the first of men
in all the chances of this life and when
we mortals have to do with more than man.
You came and by your coming saved our city,   35
freed us from tribute which we paid of old
to the Sphinx, cruel singer. This you did
in virtue of no knowledge we could give you,
in virtue of no teaching; it was God
that aided you, men say, and you are held
with God's assistance to have saved our lives.
Now Oedipus, Greatest in all men's eyes,   40
here falling at your feet we all entreat you,
find us some strength for rescue.
Perhaps you'll hear a wise word from some God,
perhaps you will learn something from a man
(for I have seen that for the skilled of practice
the outcome of their counsels live the most).   45
Noblest of men, go, and raise up our city,
go,—and give heed. For now this land of ours

calls you its savior since you saved it once.
So, let us never speak about your reign
as of a time when first our feet were set
secure on high, but later fell to ruin. 50
Raise up our city, save it and raise it up.
Once you have brought us luck with happy omen;
be no less now in fortune.
If you will rule this land, as now you rule it,
better to rule it full of men than empty. 55
For neither tower nor ship is anything
when empty, and none live in it together.

Oedipus

I pity you, children. You have come full of longing,
but I have known the story before you told it
only too well. I know you are all sick,
yet there is not one of you, sick though you are, 60
that is as sick as I myself.
Your several sorrows each have single scope
and touch but one of you. My spirit groans
for city and myself and you at once.
You have not roused me like a man from sleep; 65
know that I have given many tears to this,
gone many ways wandering in thought,
but as I thought I found only one remedy
and that I took. I sent Menoeceus' son
Creon, Jocasta's brother, to Apollo, 70
to his Pythian temple,
that he might learn there by what act or word
I could save this city. As I count the days,
it vexes me what ails him; he is gone
far longer than he needed for the journey. 75
But when he comes, then, may I prove a villain,
if I shall not do all the God commands.

Priest

 Thanks for your gracious words. Your servants here
 signal that Creon is this moment coming.

Oedipus

 His face is bright. O holy Lord Apollo,   80
 grant that his news too may be bright for us
 and bring us safety.

Priest

                It is happy news,
 I think, for else his head would not be crowned
 with sprigs of fruitful laurel.

Oedipus

                We will know soon,
 he's within hail. Lord Creon, my good brother,   85
 what is the word you bring us from the God?

                        (*Creon enters.*)

Creon

 A good word,—for things hard to bear themselves
 if in the final issue all is well
 I count complete good fortune.

Oedipus

                What do you mean?
 What you have said so far
 leaves me uncertain whether to trust or fear.   90

Creon

 If you will hear my news before these others
 I am ready to speak, or else to go within.

Oedipus
Speak it to all;
the grief I bear, I bear it more for these
than for my own heart.

Creon
                    I will tell you, then,   95
what I heard from the God.
King Phoebus in plain words commanded us
to drive out a pollution from our land,
pollution grown ingrained within the land;
drive it out, said the God, not cherish it,
till it's past cure.

Oedipus
                    What is the rite
of purification? How shall it be done?

Creon
By banishing a man, or expiation   100
of blood by blood, since it is murder guilt
which holds our city in this destroying storm.

Oedipus
Who is this man whose fate the God pronounces?

Creon
My Lord, before you piloted the state
we had a king called Laius.

Oedipus
I know of him by hearsay. I have not seen him.   105

Creon
The God commanded clearly: let some one
punish with force this dead man's murderers.

19

Oedipus

Where are they in the world? Where would a trace
of this old crime be found? It would be hard
to guess where.

Creon

                The clue is in this land;   110
that which is sought is found;
the unheeded thing escapes:
so said the God.

Oedipus

              Was it at home,
or in the country that death came upon him,
or in another country travelling?

Creon

He went, he said himself, upon an embassy,
but never returned when he set out from home.   115

Oedipus

Was there no messenger, no fellow traveller
who knew what happened? Such a one might tell
something of use.

Creon

They were all killed save one. He fled in terror
and he could tell us nothing in clear terms
of what he knew, nothing, but one thing only.

Oedipus

What was it?   120
If we could even find a slim beginning
in which to hope, we might discover much.

Creon

  This man said that the robbers they encountered
were many and the hands that did the murder
were many; it was no man's single power.

Oedipus

  How could a robber dare a deed like this
were he not helped with money from the city,
money and treachery?   125

Creon

                    That indeed was thought.
But Laius was dead and in our trouble
there was none to help.

Oedipus

  What trouble was so great to hinder you
inquiring out the murder of your king?

Creon

  The riddling Sphinx induced us to neglect   130
mysterious crimes and rather seek solution
of troubles at our feet.

Oedipus

  I will bring this to light again. King Phoebus
fittingly took this care about the dead,
and you too fittingly.
And justly you will see in me an ally,   135
a champion of my country and the God.
For when I drive pollution from the land
I will not serve a distant friend's advantage,
but act in my own interest. Whoever
he was that killed the king may readily
wish to dispatch me with the murderous hand;   140
so helping the dead king I help myself.

Come, children, take your suppliant boughs and go;
up from the altars now. Call the assembly
and let it meet upon the understanding
that I'll do everything. God will decide   145
whether we prosper or remain in sorrow.

Priest
Rise, children—it was this we came to seek,
which of himself the king now offers us.
May Phoebus who gave us the oracle
come to our rescue and stay the plague.   150

                              (*Exeunt all but the Chorus.*)

Chorus
    Strophe
What is the sweet spoken word of God from the shrine of
    Pytho rich in gold
that has come to glorious Thebes?
I am stretched on the rack of doubt, and terror and trem-
    bling hold
my heart, O Delian Healer, and I worship full of fears
for what doom you will bring to pass, new or renewed in   155
    the revolving years.
Speak to me, immortal voice,
child of golden Hope.

    Antistrophe
First I call on you, Athene, deathless daughter of Zeus,
and Artemis, Earth Upholder,   160
who sits in the midst of the market place in the throne
    which men call Fame,
and Phoebus, the Far Shooter, three averters of Fate,
come to us now, if ever before, when ruin rushed upon
    the state,   165
you drove destruction's flame away
out of our land.

Strophe

Our sorrows defy number;
all the ship's timbers are rotten;
taking of thought is no spear for the driving away of the
   plague. 170
There are no growing children in this famous land;
there are no women bearing the pangs of childbirth.
You may see them one with another, like birds swift on
   the wing, 175
quicker than fire unmastered,
speeding away to the coast of the Western God.

Antistrophe

In the unnumbered deaths
of its people the city dies;
those children that are born lie dead on the naked earth
unpitied, spreading contagion of death; and gray haired
   mothers and wives
everywhere stand at the altar's edge, suppliant, moaning; 182-
the hymn to the healing God rings out but with it the 85
   wailing voices are blended.
From these our sufferings grant us, O golden Daughter of
   Zeus,
glad-faced deliverance.

Strophe

There is no clash of brazen shields but our fight is with
   the War God,
a War God ringed with the cries of men, a savage God 191
   who burns us;
grant that he turn in racing course backwards out of our
   country's bounds
to the great palace of Amphitrite or where the waves of 195
   the Thracian sea
deny the stranger safe anchorage.
Whatsoever escapes the night

at last the light of day revisits;
so smite the War God, Father Zeus,
beneath your thunderbolt,
for you are the Lord of the lightning, the lightning that
    carries fire.   200

  Antistrophe
  And your unconquered arrow shafts, winged by the
    golden corded bow,
Lycean King, I beg to be at our side for help;   205
and the gleaming torches of Artemis with which she
    scours the Lycean hills,
and I call on the God with the turban of gold, who gave
    his name to this country of ours,   210
the Bacchic God with the wind flushed face,
Evian One, who travel
with the Maenad company,
combat the God that burns us
with your torch of pine;
for the God that is our enemy is a God unhonoured 215
    among the Gods.

                  (*Oedipus returns.*)

Oedipus
For what you ask me—if you will hear my words,
and hearing welcome them and fight the plague,
you will find strength and lightening of your load.

Hark to me; what I say to you, I say
as one that is a stranger to the story
as stranger to the deed. For I would not   220
be far upon the track if I alone
were tracing it without a clue. But now,
since after all was finished, I became
a citizen among you, citizens—
now I proclaim to all the men of Thebes:
who so among you knows the murderer   225
by whose hand Laius, son of Labdacus,

died—I command him to tell everything
to me,—yes, though he fears himself to take the blame
on his own head; for bitter punishment
he shall have none, but leave this land unharmed.
Or if he knows the murderer, another,   230
a foreigner, still let him speak the truth.
For I will pay him and be grateful, too.
But if you shall keep silence, if perhaps
some one of you, to shield a guilty friend,
or for his own sake shall reject my words—
hear what I shall do then: 235
I forbid that man, whoever he be, my land,
my land where I hold sovereignty and throne;
and I forbid any to welcome him
or cry him greeting or make him a sharer   240
in sacrifice or offering to the Gods,
or give him water for his hands to wash.
I command all to drive him from their homes,
since he is our pollution, as the oracle
of Pytho's God proclaimed him now to me.
So I stand forth a champion of the God
and of the man who died.   245
Upon the murderer I invoke this curse—
whether he is one man and all unknown,
or one of many—may he wear out his life
in misery to miserable doom!
If with my knowledge he lives at my hearth   250
I pray that I myself may feel my curse.
On you I lay my charge to fulfill all this
for me, for the God, and for this land of ours
destroyed and blighted, by the God forsaken.

Even were this no matter of God's ordinance   255
it would not fit you so to leave it lie,
unpurified, since a good man is dead
and one that was a king. Search it out.

Since I am now the holder of his office,
and have his bed and wife that once was his,   260
and had his line not been unfortunate
we would have common children—(fortune leaped
upon his head)—because of all these things,
I fight in his defence as for my father,
and I shall try all means to take the murderer   265
of Laius the son of Labdacus
the son of Polydorus and before him
of Cadmus and before him of Agenor.
Those who do not obey me, may the Gods
grant no crops springing from the ground they plough   270
nor children to their women! May a fate
like this, or one still worse than this consume them!
For you whom these words please, the other Thebans,
may Justice as your ally and all the gods
live with you, blessing you now and for ever!   275

Chorus
    As you have held me to my oath, I speak:
    I neither killed the king nor can declare
    the killer; but since Phoebus set the quest
    it is his part to tell who the man is.

Oedipus
    Right; but to put compulsion on the Gods   280
    against their will—no man can do that.

Chorus
    May I then say what I think second best?

Oedipus
    If there's a third best, too, spare not to tell it.

Chorus
    I know that what the Lord Teiresias
    sees, is most often what the Lord Apollo   285

sees. If you should inquire of this from him
you might find out most clearly.

Oedipus
Even in this my actions have not been sluggard.
On Creon's word I have sent two messengers
and why the prophet is not here already
I have been wondering.

Chorus
His skill apart   290
there is besides only an old faint story.

Oedipus
What is it?
I look at every story.

Chorus
It was said
that he was killed by certain wayfarers.

Oedipus
I heard that, too, but no one saw the killer.

Chorus
Yet if he has a share of fear at all,
his courage will not stand firm, hearing your curse.   295

Oedipus
The man who in the doing did not shrink
will fear no word.

Chorus
Here comes his prosecutor:
led by your men the godly prophet comes
in whom alone of mankind truth is native.

(Enter Teiresias, led by a little boy.)

Oedipus

Teiresias, you are versed in everything, 300
things teachable and things not to be spoken,
things of the heaven and earth-creeping things.
You have no eyes but in your mind you know
with what a plague our city is afflicted.
My lord, in you alone we find a champion,
in you alone one that can rescue us.
Perhaps you have not heard the messengers, 305
but Phoebus sent in answer to our sending
an oracle declaring that our freedom
from this disease would only come when we
should learn the names of those who killed King Laius,
and kill them or expel from our country.
Do not begrudge us oracles from birds, 310
or any other way of prophecy
within your skill; save yourself and the city,
save me; redeem the debt of our pollution
that lies on us because of this dead man.
We are in your hands; pains are most nobly taken
to help another when you have means and power. 315

Teiresias

Alas, how terrible is wisdom when
it brings no profit to the man that's wise!
This I knew well, but had forgotten it,
else I would not have come here.

Oedipus

What is this?
How sad you are now you have come!

Teiresias

Let me
go home. It will be easiest for us both 320

28

to bear our several destinies to the end
if you will follow my advice.

Oedipus

You'd rob us
of this your gift of prophecy? You talk
as one who had no care for law nor love
for Thebes who reared you.

Teiresias

Yes, but I see that even your own words
miss the mark; therefore I must fear for mine.   325

Oedipus

For God's sake if you know of anything,
do not turn from us; all of us kneel to you,
all of us here, your suppliants.

Teiresias

All of you here know nothing. I will not
bring to the light of day my troubles, mine—
rather than call them yours.

Oedipus

What do you mean?
You know of something but refuse to speak.
Would you betray us and destroy the city?   330

Teiresias

I will not bring this pain upon us both,
neither on you nor on myself. Why is it
you question me and waste your labour? I
will tell you nothing.

29

Oedipus

You would provoke a stone! Tell us, you villain,   335
tell us, and do not stand there quietly
unmoved and balking at the issue.

Teiresias

You blame my temper but you do not see
your own that lives within you; it is me
you chide.

Oedipus

Who would not feel his temper rise
at words like these with which you shame our city?   340

Teiresias

Of themselves things will come, although I hide them
and breathe no word of them.

Oedipus

Since they will come

tell them to me.

Teiresias

I will say nothing further.
Against this answer let your temper rage
as wildly as you will.

Oedipus

Indeed I am   345
so angry I shall not hold back a jot
of what I think. For I would have you know
I think you were complotter of the deed
and doer of the deed save in so far
as for the actual killing. Had you had eyes
I would have said alone you murdered him.

Teiresias
Yes? Then I warn you faithfully to keep   350
the letter of your proclamation and
from this day forth to speak no word of greeting
to these nor me; you are the land's pollution.

Oedipus
How shamelessly you started up this taunt!
How do you think you will escape?   355

Teiresias
                    I have.
I have escaped; the truth is what I cherish
and that's my strength.

Oedipus
                    And who has taught you truth?
Not your profession surely!

Teiresias
                    You have taught me,
for you have made me speak against my will.

Oedipus
Speak what? Tell me again that I may learn it better.

Teiresias
Did you not understand before or would you
provoke me into speaking?   360

Oedipus
                    I did not grasp it,
not so to call it known. Say it again.

Teiresias
I say you are the murderer of the king
whose murderer you seek.

Oedipus

           Not twice you shall
say calumnies like this and stay unpunished.

Teiresias

Shall I say more to tempt your anger more?

Oedipus

As much as you desire; it will be said   365
in vain.

Teiresias

          I say that with those you love best
you live in foulest shame unconsciously
and do not see where you are in calamity.

Oedipus

Do you imagine you can always talk
like this, and live to laugh at it hereafter?

Teiresias

Yes, if the truth has anything of strength.

Oedipus

It has, but not for you; it has no strength   370
for you because you are blind in mind and ears
as well as in your eyes.

Teiresias

          You are a poor wretch
to taunt me with the very insults which
every one soon will heap upon yourself.

Oedipus

Your life is one long night so that you cannot
hurt me or any other who sees the light.   375

Teiresias
  It is not fate that I should be your ruin,
  Apollo is enough; it is his care
  to work this out.

Oedipus
                    Was this your own design
    or Creon's?

Teiresias
                    Creon is no hurt to you,
    but you are to yourself.

Oedipus
  Wealth, sovereignty and skill outmatching skill   380
  for the contrivance of an envied life!
  Great store of jealousy fill your treasury chests,
  if my friend Creon, friend from the first and loyal,   385
  thus secretly attacks me, secretly
  desires to drive me out and secretly
  suborns this juggling, trick devising quack,
  this wily beggar who has only eyes
  for his own gains, but blindness in his skill.
  For, tell me, where have you seen clear, Teiresias,   390
  with your prophetic eyes? When the dark singer,
  the sphinx, was in your country, did you speak
  word of deliverance to its citizens?
  And yet the riddle's answer was not the province
  of a chance comer. It was a prophet's task
  and plainly you had no such gift of prophecy   395
  from birds nor otherwise from any God
  to glean a word of knowledge. But I came,
  Oedipus, who knew nothing, and I stopped her.
  I solved the riddle by my wit alone.
  Mine was no knowledge got from birds. And now
  you would expel me,

because you think that you will find a place   400
by Creon's throne. I think you will be sorry,
both you and your accomplice, for your plot
to drive me out. And did I not regard you
as an old man, some suffering would have taught you
that what was in your heart was treason.

Chorus

We look at this man's words and yours, my king,
and we find both have spoken them in anger.   405
We need no angry words but only thought
how we may best hit the God's meaning for us.

Teiresias

If you are king, at least I have the right
no less to speak in my defence against you.
Of that much I am master. I am no slave   410
of yours, but Loxias', and so I shall not
enroll myself with Creon for my patron.
Since you have taunted me with being blind,
here is my word for you.
You have your eyes but see not where you are
in sin, nor where you live, nor whom you live with.
Do you know who your parents are? Unknowing   415
you are an enemy to kith and kin
in death, beneath the earth, and in this life.
A deadly footed, double striking curse,
from father and mother both, shall drive you forth
out of this land, with darkness on your eyes,
that now have such straight vision. Shall there be
a place will not be harbour to your cries,   420
a corner of Cithaeron will not ring
in echo to your cries, soon, soon,—
when you shall learn the secret of your marriage,
which steered you to a haven in this house,—
haven no haven, after lucky voyage?

34

And of the multitude of other evils
establishing a grim equality
between you and your children, you know nothing.   425
So, muddy with contempt my words and Creon's!
Misery shall grind no man as it will you.

Oedipus
Is it endurable that I should hear
such words from him? Go and a curse go with you!   430
Quick, home with you! Out of my house at once!

Teiresias
I would not have come either had you not called me.

Oedipus
I did not know then you would talk like a fool—
or it would have been long before I called you.

Teiresias
I am a fool then, as it seems to you—   435
but to the parents who have bred you, wise.

Oedipus
What parents? Stop! Who are they of all the world?

Teiresias
This day will show your birth and will destroy you.

Oedipus
How needlessly your riddles darken everything.

Teiresias
But it's in riddle answering you are strongest.   440

Oedipus
Yes. Taunt me where you will find me great.

Teiresias
It is this very luck that has destroyed you.

35

Oedipus

I do not care, if it has saved this city.

Teiresias

Well, I will go. Come, boy, lead me away.

Oedipus

Yes, lead him off. So long as you are here,   445
you'll be a stumbling block and a vexation;
once gone, you will not trouble me again.

Teiresias

             I have said
what I came here to say not fearing your
countenance: there is no way you can hurt me.
I tell you, king, this man, this murderer
(whom you have long declared you are in search of,
indicting him in threatening proclamation   450
as murderer of Laius)—he is here.
In name he is a stranger among citizens
but soon he will be shown to be a citizen
true native Theban, and he'll have no joy
of the discovery: blindness for sight
and beggary for riches his exchange,   455
he shall go journeying to a foreign country
tapping his way before him with a stick.
He shall be proved father and brother both
to his own children in his house; to her
that gave him birth, a son and husband both;
a fellow sower in his father's bed
with that same father that he murdered.
Go within, reckon that out, and if you find me   460
mistaken, say I have no skill in prophecy.

(Exeunt separately Teiresias and Oedipus.)

Chorus

Strophe

Who is the man proclaimed
by Delphi's prophetic rock
as the bloody handed murderer,   465
the doer of deeds that none dare name?
Now is the time for him to run
with a stronger foot
than Pegasus
for the child of Zeus leaps in arms upon him   470
with fire and the lightning bolt,
and terribly close on his heels
are the Fates that never miss.

Antistrophe

Lately from snowy Parnassus
clearly the voice flashed forth,
bidding each Theban track him down,   475
the unknown murderer.
In the savage forests he lurks and in
the caverns like
the mountain bull.
He is sad and lonely, and lonely his feet
that carry him far from the navel of earth;   480
but its prophecies, ever living,
flutter around his head.

Strophe

The augur has spread confusion,
terrible confusion;
I do not approve what was said   485
nor can I deny it.
I do not know what to say;
I am in a flutter of foreboding;
I never heard in the present
nor past of a quarrel between   490

37

the sons of Labdacus and Polybus,
that I might bring as proof
in attacking the popular fame
of Oedipus, seeking
to take vengeance for undiscovered
death in the line of Labdacus. 495

Antistrophe

Truly Zeus and Apollo are wise
and in human things all knowing;
but amongst men there is no 500
distinct judgment, between the prophet
and me—which of us is right.
One man may pass another in wisdom
but I would never agree
with those that find fault with the king
till I should see the word
proved right beyond doubt. For once
in visible form the Sphinx
came on him and all of us
saw his wisdom and in that test
he saved the city. So he will not be condemned by my
    mind. 512

(Enter Creon.)

Creon

Citizens, I have come because I heard
deadly words spread about me, that the king
accuses me. I cannot take that from him.
If he believes that in these present troubles 515
he has been wronged by me in word or deed
I do not want to live on with the burden
of such a scandal on me. The report 520
injures me doubly and most vitally—
for I'll be called a traitor to my city
and traitor also to my friends and you.

Chorus
Perhaps it was a sudden gust of anger
that forced that insult from him, and no judgment.

Creon
But did he say that it was in compliance   525
with schemes of mine that the seer told him lies?

Chorus
Yes, he said that, but why, I do not know.

Creon
Were his eyes straight in his head? Was his mind right
when he accused me in this fashion?

Chorus
I do not know; I have no eyes to see   530
what princes do. Here comes the king himself.

(*Enter Oedipus.*)

Oedipus
You, sir, how is it you come here? Have you so much
brazen-faced daring that you venture in
my house although you are proved manifestly
the murderer of that man, and though you tried,
openly, highway robbery of my crown?   535
For God's sake, tell me what you saw in me,
what cowardice or what stupidity,
that made you lay a plot like this against me?
Did you imagine I should not observe
the crafty scheme that stole upon me or
seeing it, take no means to counter it?   540
Was it not stupid of you to make the attempt,
to try to hunt down royal power without
the people at your back or friends? For only

39

with the people at your back or money can
the hunt end in the capture of a crown.

Creon

Do you know what you're doing? Will you listen
to words to answer yours, and then pass judgment?

Oedipus

You're quick to speak, but I am slow to grasp you,   545
for I have found you dangerous,—and my foe.

Creon

First of all hear what I shall say to that.

Oedipus

At least don't tell me that you are not guilty.

Creon

If you think obstinacy without wisdom
a valuable possession, you are wrong.   550

Oedipus

And you are wrong if you believe that one,
a criminal, will not be punished only
because he is my kinsman.

Creon

                    This is but just—
but tell me, then, of what offense I'm guilty?

Oedipus

Did you or did you not urge me to send   555
to this prophetic mumbler?

Creon

                    I did indeed,
and I shall stand by what I told you.

Oedipus
How long ago is it since Laius. . . .

Creon
What about Laius? I don't understand.

Oedipus
Vanished—died—was murdered?   560

Creon
                    It is long,
a long, long time to reckon.

Oedipus
                    Was this prophet
in the profession then?

Creon
                    He was, and honoured
as highly as he is today.

Oedipus
At that time did he say a word about me?

Creon
Never, at least when I was near him.   565

Oedipus
You never made a search for the dead man?

Creon
We searched, indeed, but never learned of anything.

Oedipus
Why did our wise old friend not say this then?

Creon

I don't know; and when I know nothing, I
usually hold my tongue.

Oedipus

You know this much,   570
and can declare this much if you are loyal.

Creon

What is it? If I know, I'll not deny it.

Oedipus

That he would not have said that I killed Laius
had he not met you first.

Creon

You know yourself
whether he said this, but I demand that I   575
should hear as much from you as you from me.

Oedipus

Then hear,—I'll not be proved a murderer.

Creon

Well, then. You're married to my sister.

Oedipus

Yes,
that I am not disposed to deny.

Creon

You rule
this country giving her an equal share
in the government?

42

Oedipus
>   Yes, everything she wants   580
> she has from me.

Creon
>   And I, as thirdsman to you,
> am rated as the equal of you two?

Oedipus
> Yes, and it's there you've proved yourself false friend.

Creon
> Not if you will reflect on it as I do.
> Consider, first, if you think any one
> would choose to rule and fear rather than rule   585
> and sleep untroubled by a fear if power
> were equal in both cases. I, at least,
> I was not born with such a frantic yearning
> to be a king—but to do what kings do.
> And so it is with every one who has learned
> wisdom and self-control. As it stands now,
> the prizes are all mine—and without fear.   590
> But if I were the king myself, I must
> do much that went against the grain.
> How should despotic rule seem sweeter to me
> than painless power and an assured authority?
> I am not so besotted yet that I
> want other honours than those that come with profit.   595
> Now every man's my pleasure; every man greets me;
> now those who are your suitors fawn on me,—
> success for them depends upon my favour.
> Why should I let all this go to win that?
> My mind would not be traitor if it's wise;   600
> I am no treason lover, of my nature,
> nor would I ever dare to join a plot.
> Prove what I say. Go to the oracle

at Pytho and inquire about the answers,
if they are as I told you. For the rest,   605
if you discover I laid any plot
together with the seer, kill me, I say,
not only by your vote but by my own.
But do not charge me on obscure opinion
without some proof to back it. It's not just
lightly to count your knaves as honest men,   610
nor honest men as knaves. To throw away
an honest friend is, as it were, to throw
your life away, which a man loves the best.
In time you will know all with certainty;
time is the only test of honest men,
one day is space enough to know a rogue.   615

Chorus

His words are wise, king, if one fears to fall.
Those who are quick of temper are not safe.

Oedipus

When he that plots against me secretly
moves quickly, I must quickly counterplot.
If I wait taking no decisive measure   620
his business will be done, and mine be spoiled.

Creon

What do you want to do then? Banish me?

Oedipus

No, certainly; kill you, not banish you.[1]

1. Two lines omitted here owing to the confusion in the dialogue consequent on the loss of a third line. The lines as they stand in Jebb's edition (1902) are:
Oed.: That you may show what manner of thing is envy.
Creon: You speak as one that will not yield or trust.
[*Oed.* lost line.]

Creon
I do not think that you've your wits about you. 626

Oedipus
For my own interests, yes.

Creon
                    But for mine, too,
you should think equally.

Oedipus
                    You are a rogue.

Creon
Suppose you do not understand?

Oedipus
                    But yet
I must be ruler.

Creon
                    Not if you rule badly.

Oedipus
O, city, city!

Creon
                    I too have some share 630
in the city; it is not yours alone.

Chorus
Stop, my lords! Here—and in the nick of time
I see Jocasta coming from the house;
with her help lay the quarrel that now stirs you.

(*Enter Jocasta.*)

Jocasta

For shame! Why have you raised this foolish squabbling
brawl? Are you not ashamed to air your private   635
griefs when the country's sick? Go in, you, Oedipus,
and you, too, Creon, into the house. Don't magnify
your nothing troubles.

Creon

               Sister, Oedipus,
your husband, thinks he has the right to do
terrible wrongs—he has but to choose between   640
two terrors: banishing or killing me.

Oedipus

He's right, Jocasta; for I find him plotting
with knavish tricks against my person.

Creon

That God may never bless me! May I die
accursed, if I have been guilty of   645
one tittle of the charge you bring against me!

Jocasta

I beg you, Oedipus, trust him in this,
spare him for the sake of this his oath to God,
for my sake, and the sake of those who stand here.

Chorus

Be gracious, be merciful,   649
we beg of you.

Oedipus

In what would you have me yield?

46

Chorus
He has been no silly child in the past.
He is strong in his oath now.
Spare him.

Oedipus
Do you know what you ask?

Chorus
Yes.

Oedipus
Tell me then.

Chorus
He has been your friend before all men's eyes; do not   656
cast him away dishonoured on an obscure conjecture.

Oedipus
I would have you know that this request of yours
really requests my death or banishment.

Chorus
May the Sun God, king of Gods, forbid! May I die with-   660
out God's blessing, without friends' help, if I had any
such thought. But my spirit is broken by my unhappiness   663
for my wasting country; and this would but add troubles
amongst ourselves to the other troubles.

Oedipus
Well, let him go then—if I must die ten times for it,   669
or be sent out dishonoured into exile.
It is your lips that prayed for him I pitied,
not his; wherever he is, I shall hate him.

Creon
I see you sulk in yielding and you're dangerous
when you are out of temper; natures like yours
are justly heaviest for themselves to bear.   675

Oedipus
Leave me alone! Take yourself off, I tell you.

Creon
I'll go, you have not known me, but they have,
and they have known my innocence.

(*Exit.*)

Chorus
Won't you take him inside, lady?

Jocasta
Yes, when I've found out what was the matter.

Chorus
There was some misconceived suspicion of a story, and on
the other side the sting of injustice.

Jocasta
So, on both sides?

Chorus
Yes.

Jocasta
What was the story?

Chorus
I think it best, in the interests of the country, to leave it   685
where it ended.

Oedipus

You see where you have ended, straight of judgment
although you are, by softening my anger.

Chorus

Sir, I have said before and I say again—be sure that I   689
would have been proved a madman, bankrupt in sane
council, if I should put you away, you who steered the
country I love safely when she was crazed with troubles.   695
God grant that now, too, you may prove a fortunate guide
for us.

Jocasta

Tell me, my lord, I beg of you, what was it
that roused your anger so?

Oedipus

           Yes, I will tell you.   700
I honour you more than I honour them.
It was Creon and the plots he laid against me.

Jocasta

Tell me—if you can clearly tell the quarrel—

Oedipus

          Creon says
that I'm the murderer of Laius.

Jocasta

Of his own knowledge or on information?

Oedipus

He sent this rascal prophet to me, since   705
he keeps his own mouth clean of any guilt.

Jocasta

Do not concern yourself about this matter;
listen to me and learn that human beings

49

have no part in the craft of prophecy.
Of that I'll show you a short proof.   710
There was an oracle once that came to Laius,—
I will not say that it was Phoebus' own,
but it was from his servants—and it told him
that it was fate that he should die a victim
at the hands of his own son, a son to be born
of Laius and me. But, see now, he,
the king, was killed by foreign highway robbers   715
at a place where three roads meet—so goes the story;
and for the son—before three days were out
after his birth King Laius pierced his ankles
and by the hands of others cast him forth
upon a pathless hillside. So Apollo   720
failed to fulfill his oracle to the son,
that he should kill his father, and to Laius
also proved false in that the thing he feared,
death at his son's hands, never came to pass.
So clear in this case were the oracles,
so clear and false. Give them no heed, I say;
what God discovers need of, easily
he shows to us himself.   725

Oedipus

                    O dear Jocasta,
as I hear this from you, there comes upon me
a wandering of the soul—I could run mad.

Jocasta

What trouble is it, that you turn again
and speak like this?

Oedipus

                    I thought I heard you say
that Laius was killed at a crossroads.   730

Jocasta
  Yes, that was how the story went and still
  that word goes round.

Oedipus
                    Where is this place, Jocasta,
  where he was murdered?

Jocasta
                    Phocis is the country
  and the road splits there, one of two roads from Delphi,
  another comes from Daulia.

Oedipus
                    How long ago is this?   735

Jocasta
  The news came to the city just before
  you became king and all men's eyes looked to you.
  What is it, Oedipus, that's in your mind?

Oedipus
  What have you designed, O Zeus, to do with me?

Jocasta
  What is the thought that troubles your heart?

Oedipus
  Don't ask me yet—tell me of Laius—   740
  How did he look? How old or young was he?

Jocasta
  He was a tall man and his hair was grizzled
  already—nearly white—and in his form
  not unlike you.

Oedipus

O God, I think I have
called curses on myself in ignorance. 745

Jocasta

What do you mean? I am terrified
when I look at you.

Oedipus

I have a deadly fear
that the old seer had eyes. You'll show me more
if you can tell me one more thing.

Jocasta

I will.
I'm frightened,—but if I can understand,
I'll tell you all you ask.

Oedipus

How was his company? 750
Had he few with him when he went this journey,
or many servants, as would suit a prince?

Jocasta

In all there were but five, and among them
a herald; and one carriage for the king.

Oedipus

It's plain—it's plain—who was it told you this? 755

Jocasta

The only servant that escaped safe home.

Oedipus

Is he at home now?

52

Jocasta
No, when he came home again
and saw you king and Laius was dead,
he came to me and touched my hand and begged   760
that I should send him to the fields to be
my shepherd and so he might see the city
as far off as he might. So I
sent him away. He was an honest man,
as slaves go, and was worthy of far more
than what he asked of me.

Oedipus
O, how I wish that he could come back quickly!   765

Jocasta
He can. Why is your heart so set on this?

Oedipus
O dear Jocasta, I am full of fears
that I have spoken far too much; and therefore
I wish to see this shepherd.

Jocasta
He will come;
but, Oedipus, I think I'm worthy too
to know what it is that disquiets you.   770

Oedipus
It shall not be kept from you, since my mind
has gone so far with its forebodings. Whom
should I confide in rather than you, who is there
of more importance to me who have passed
through such a fortune?
Polybus was my father, king of Corinth,
and Merope, the Dorian, my mother.   775
I was held greatest of the citizens
in Corinth till a curious chance befell me

53

as I shall tell you—curious, indeed,
but hardly worth the store I set upon it.
There was a dinner and at it a man,
a drunken man, accused me in his drink   780
of being bastard. I was furious
but held my temper under for that day.
Next day I went and taxed my parents with it;
they took the insult very ill from him,
the drunken fellow who had uttered it.
So I was comforted for their part, but   785
still this thing rankled always, for the story
crept about widely. And I went at last
to Pytho, though my parents did not know.
But Phoebus sent me home again unhonoured
in what I came to learn, but he foretold   790
other and desperate horrors to befall me,
that I was fated to lie with my mother,
and show to daylight an accursed breed
which men would not endure, and I was doomed
to be murderer of the father that begot me.
When I heard this I fled, and in the days
that followed I would measure from the stars   795
the whereabouts of Corinth—yes, I fled
to somewhere where I should not see fulfilled
the infamies told in that dreadful oracle.
And as I journeyed I came to the place
where, as you say, this king met with his death.
Jocasta, I will tell you the whole truth.   800
When I was near the branching of the crossroads,
going on foot, I was encountered by
a herald and a carriage with a man in it,
just as you tell me. He that led the way
and the old man himself wanted to thrust me   805
out of the road by force. I became angry
and struck the coachman who was pushing me.
When the old man saw this he watched his moment,

and as I passed he struck me from his carriage,
full on the head with his two pointed goad.
But he was paid in full and presently   810
my stick had struck him backwards from the car
and he rolled out of it. And then I killed them
all. If it happened there was any tie
of kinship twixt this man and Laius,
who is then now more miserable than I,   815
what man on earth so hated by the Gods,
since neither citizen nor foreigner
may welcome me at home or even greet me,
but drive me out of doors? And it is I,
I and no other have so cursed myself.   820
And I pollute the bed of him I killed
by the hands that killed him. Was I not born evil?
Am I not utterly unclean? I had to fly
and in my banishment not even see
my kindred nor set foot in my own country,
or otherwise my fate was to be yoked   825
in marriage with my mother and kill my father,
Polybus who begot me and had reared me.
Would not one rightly judge and say that on me
these things were sent by some malignant God?
O no, no, no—O holy majesty   830
of God on high, may I not see that day!
May I be gone out of men's sight before
I see the deadly taint of this disaster
come upon me.

Chorus

Sir, we too fear these things. But until you see this man
face to face and hear his story, hope.   835

Oedipus

Yes, I have just this much of hope—to wait until the
herdsman comes.

Jocasta

And when he comes, what do you want with him?

Oedipus

I'll tell you; if I find that his story is the same as yours,
I at least will be clear of this guilt.   840

Jocasta

Why what so particularly did you learn from my story?

Oedipus

You said that he spoke of highway *robbers* who killed
Laius. Now if he uses the same number, it was not I who
killed him. One man cannot be the same as many. But if   845
he speaks of a man travelling alone, then clearly the
burden of the guilt inclines towards me.

Jocasta

Be sure, at least, that this was how he told the story. He
cannot unsay it now, for every one in the city heard it—   850
not I alone. But, Oedipus, even if he diverges from what
he said then, he shall never prove that the murder of
Laius squares rightly with the prophecy—for Loxias declared that the king should be killed by his own son. And
that poor creature did not kill him surely,—for he died   855
himself first. So as far as prophecy goes, henceforward I
shall not look to the right hand or the left.

Oedipus

Right. But yet, send some one for the peasant to bring   860
him here; do not neglect it.

Jocasta

I will send quickly. Now let me go indoors. I will do nothing except what pleases you.

(*Exeunt.*)

56

Chorus

Strophe

May destiny ever find me
pious in word and deed   865
prescribed by the laws that live on high:
laws begotten in the clear air of heaven,
whose only father is Olympus;
no mortal nature brought them to birth,
no forgetfulness shall lull them to sleep;   870
for God is great in them and grows not old.

Antistrophe

Insolence breeds the tyrant, insolence
if it is glutted with a surfeit, unseasonable, unprofitable,   875
climbs to the roof-top and plunges
sheer down to the ruin that must be,
and there its feet are no service.
But I pray that the God may never   880
abolish the eager ambition that profits the state.
For I shall never cease to hold the God as our protector.

Strophe

If a man walks with haughtiness
of hand or word and gives no heed   885
to Justice and the shrines of Gods
despises—may an evil doom
smite him for his ill-starred pride of heart!—
if he reaps gains without justice
and will not hold from impiety   890
and his fingers itch for untouchable things.
When such things are done, what man shall contrive
to shield his soul from the shafts of the God?
When such deeds are held in honour,   895
why should I honour the Gods in the dance?

Antistrophe

No longer to the holy place,
to the navel of earth I'll go
to worship, nor to Abae
nor to Olympia,   900
unless the oracles are proved to fit,
for all men's hands to point at.
O Zeus, if you are rightly called
the sovereign lord, all-mastering,
let this not escape you nor your ever-living power!   905
The oracles concerning Laius
are old and dim and men regard them not.
Apollo is nowhere clear in honour; God's service perishes.   910

(Enter Jocasta, carrying garlands.)

Jocasta

Princes of the land, I have had the thought to go
to the Gods' temples, bringing in my hand
garlands and gifts of incense, as you see.
For Oedipus excites himself too much
at every sort of trouble, not conjecturing,   915
like a man of sense, what will be from what was,
but he is always at the speaker's mercy,
when he speaks terrors. I can do no good
by my advice, and so I came as suppliant
to you, Lycaean Apollo, who are nearest.
These are the symbols of my prayer and this   920
my prayer: grant us escape free of the curse.
Now when we look to him we are all afraid;
he's pilot of our ship and he is frightened.

(Enter Messenger.)

Messenger

Might I learn from you, sirs, where is the house of   925
Oedipus? Or best of all, if you know, where is the king
himself?

Chorus
This is his house and he is within doors. This lady is his
wife and mother of his children.

Messenger
God bless you, lady, and God bless your household! God   930
bless Oedipus' noble wife!

Jocasta
God bless you, sir, for your kind greeting! What do you
want of us that you have come here? What have you to
tell us?

Messenger
Good news, lady. Good for your house and for your
husband.

Jocasta
What is your news? Who sent you to us?   935

Messenger
I come from Corinth and the news I bring will give you
pleasure. Perhaps a little pain too.

Jocasta
What is this news of double meaning?

Messenger
The people of the Isthmus will choose Oedipus to be   940
their king. That is the rumour there.

Jocasta
But isn't their king still old Polybus?

Messenger
No. He is in his grave. Death has got him.

59

Jocasta
Is that the truth? Is Oedipus' father dead?

Messenger
May I die myself if it be otherwise!

Jocasta   (*to a servant.*)
Be quick and run to the king with the news! O oracles of   945
the Gods, where are you now? It was from this man
Oedipus fled, lest he should be his murderer! And now he
is dead, in the course of nature, and not killed by
Oedipus.

                                                    (*Enter Oedipus.*)
Oedipus
Dearest Jocasta, why have you sent for me?   950

Jocasta
Listen to this man and when you hear reflect what is the
outcome of the holy oracles of the Gods.

Oedipus
Who is he? What is his message for me?

Jocasta
He is from Corinth and he tells us that your father   955
Polybus is dead and gone.

Oedipus
What's this you say, sir? Tell me yourself.

Messenger
Since this is the first matter you want clearly told:
Polybus has gone down to death. You may be sure of it.

Oedipus
   By treachery or sickness?   960

Messenger
   A small thing will put old bodies asleep.

Oedipus
   So he died of sickness, it seems,—poor old man!

Messenger
   Yes, and of age—the long years he had measured.

Oedipus
   Ha! Ha! O dear Jocasta, why should one
   look to the Pythian hearth? Why should one look   965
   to the birds screaming overhead? They prophesied
   that I should kill my father! But he's dead,
   and hidden deep in earth, and I stand here
   who never laid a hand on spear against him,—
   unless perhaps he died of longing for me,
   and thus I am his murderer. But they,   970
   the oracles, as they stand—he's taken them
   away with him, they're dead as he himself is,
   and worthless.

Jocasta
                 That I told you before now.

Oedipus
   You did, but I was misled by my fear.

Jocasta
   Then lay no more of them to heart, not one.   975

Oedipus
   But surely I must fear my mother's bed?

Jocasta
Why should man fear since chance is all in all
for him, and he can clearly foreknow nothing?
Best to live lightly, as one can, unthinkingly.
As to your mother's marriage bed,—don't fear it.   980
Before this, in dreams too, as well as oracles,
many a man has lain with his own mother.
But he to whom such things are nothing bears
his life most easily.

Oedipus
All that you say would be said perfectly
if she were dead; but since she lives I must   985
still fear, although you talk so well, Jocasta.

Jocasta
Still in your father's death there's light of comfort?

Oedipus
Great light of comfort; but I fear the living.

Messenger
Who is the woman that makes you afraid?

Oedipus
Merope, old man, Polybus' wife.   990

Messenger
What about her frightens the queen and you?

Oedipus
A terrible oracle, stranger, from the Gods.

Messenger
Can it be told? Or does the sacred law
forbid another to have knowledge of it?

Oedipus

O no! Once on a time Loxias said
that I should lie with my own mother and   995
take on my hands the blood of my own father.
And so for these long years I've lived away
from Corinth; it has been to my great happiness;
but yet it's sweet to see the face of parents.

Messenger

This was the fear which drove you out of Corinth?   1000

Oedipus

Old man, I did not wish to kill my father.

Messenger

Why should I not free you from this fear, sir,
since I have come to you in all goodwill?

Oedipus

You would not find me thankless if you did.

Messenger

Why, it was just for this I brought the news,—   1005
to earn your thanks when you had come safe home.

Oedipus

No, I will never come near my parents.

Messenger

                    Son,
it's very plain you don't know what you're doing.

Oedipus

What do you mean, old man? For God's sake, tell me.

Messenger

If your homecoming is checked by fears like these.   1010

Oedipus
Yes, I'm afraid that Phoebus may prove right.

Messenger
The murder and the incest?

Oedipus
                Yes, old man;
that is my constant terror.

Messenger
                Do you know
that all your fears are empty?

Oedipus
                How is that,   1015
if they are father and mother and I their son?

Messenger
Because Polybus was no kin to you in blood.

Oedipus
What, was not Polybus my father?

Messenger
No more than I but just so much.

Oedipus
             How can
my father be my father as much as one
that's nothing to me?

Messenger
                Neither he nor I   1020
begat you.

Oedipus

Why then did he call me son?

Messenger
A gift he took you from these hands of mine.

Oedipus
Did he love so much what he took from another's hand?

Messenger
His childlessness before persuaded him.

Oedipus
Was I a child you bought or found when I   1025
was given to him?

Messenger
On Cithaeron's slopes
in the twisting thickets you were found.

Oedipus
And why
were you a traveller in those parts?

Messenger
I was
in charge of mountain flocks.

Oedipus
You were a shepherd?
A hireling vagrant?

Messenger
Yes, but at least at that time   1030
the man that saved your life, son.

Oedipus
What ailed me when you took me in your arms?

Messenger
In that your ankles should be witnesses.

Oedipus
Why do you speak of that old pain?

Messenger
     I loosed you;
the tendons of your feet were pierced and fettered,—

Oedipus
My swaddling clothes brought me a rare disgrace.   1035

Messenger
So that from this you're called your present name.

Oedipus
Was this my father's doing or my mother's?
For God's sake, tell me.

Messenger
     I don't know, but he
who gave you to me has more knowledge than I.

Oedipus
You yourself did not find me then? You took me
from someone else?

Messenger
    Yes, from another shepherd.   1040

Oedipus
Who was he? Do you know him well enough
to tell?

66

Messenger

He was called Laius' man.

Oedipus

You mean the king who reigned here in the old days?

Messenger

Yes, he was that man's shepherd.

Oedipus

Is he alive 1045
still, so that I could see him?

Messenger

You who live here
would know that best.

Oedipus

Do any of you here
know of this shepherd whom he speaks about
in town or in the fields? Tell me. It's time 1050
that this was found out once for all.

Chorus

I think he is none other than the peasant
whom you have sought to see already; but
Jocasta here can tell us best of that.

Oedipus

Jocasta, do you know about this man
whom we have sent for? Is he the man he mentions? 1055

Jocasta

Why ask of whom he spoke? Don't give it heed;
nor try to keep in mind what has been said.
It will be wasted labour.

Oedipus

With such clues
I could not fail to bring my birth to light.

Jocasta

I beg you—do not hunt this out—I beg you,   1060
if you have any care for your own life.
What I am suffering is enough.

Oedipus

Keep up
your heart, Jocasta. Though I'm proved a slave,
thrice slave, and though my mother is thrice slave,
you'll not be shown to be of lowly lineage.

Jocasta

O be persuaded by me, I entreat you;
do not do this.

Oedipus

I will not be persuaded to let be   1065
the chance of finding out the whole thing clearly.

Jocasta

It is because I wish you well that I
give you this counsel—and it's the best counsel.

Oedipus

Then the best counsel vexes me, and has
for some while since.

Jocasta

O Oedipus, God help you!
God keep you from the knowledge of who you are!

Oedipus

Here, some one, go and fetch the shepherd for me;
and let her find her joy in her rich family!   1070

Jocasta

O Oedipus, unhappy Oedipus!
that is all I can call you, and the last thing
that I shall ever call you.

(*Exit.*)

Chorus

Why has the queen gone, Oedipus, in wild
grief rushing from us? I am afraid that trouble   1075
will break out of this silence.

Oedipus

Break out what will! I at least shall be
willing to see my ancestry, though humble.
Perhaps she is ashamed of my low birth,
for she has all a woman's high-flown pride.
But I account myself a child of Fortune,   1080
beneficent Fortune, and I shall not be
dishonoured. She's the mother from whom I spring;
the months, my brothers, marked me, now as small,
and now again as mighty. Such is my breeding,
and I shall never prove so false to it,   1085
as not to find the secret of my birth.

Chorus

Strophe

If I am a prophet and wise of heart
you shall not fail, Cithaeron,   1090
by the limitless sky, you shall not!—
to know at tomorrow's full moon
that Oedipus honours you,

69

as native to him and mother and nurse at once;
and that you are honoured in dancing by us, as finding
    favour in sight of our king.
Apollo, to whom we cry, find these things pleasing!

  Antistrophe
Who was it bore you, child? One of   1098
the long-lived nymphs who lay with Pan—
the father who treads the hills?
Or was she a bride of Loxias, your mother? The grassy
    slopes
are all of them dear to him. Or perhaps Cyllene's king   1104
or the Bacchants' God that lives on the tops
of the hills received you a gift from some
one of the Helicon Nymphs, with whom he mostly plays?

(*Enter an old man, led by Oedipus' servants.*)

Oedipus
If some one like myself who never met him   1110
may make a guess,—I think this is the herdsman,
whom we were seeking. His old age is consonant
with the other. And besides, the men who bring him
I recognize as my own servants. You   1115
perhaps may better me in knowledge since
you've seen the man before.

Chorus
           You can be sure
I recognize him. For if Laius
had ever an honest shepherd, this was he.

Oedipus
You, sir, from Corinth, I must ask you first,
is this the man you spoke of?   1120

Messenger
> This is he
before your eyes.

Oedipus
> Old man, look here at me
and tell me what I ask you. Were you ever
a servant of King Laius?

Herdsman
> I was,—
no slave he bought but reared in his own house.

Oedipus
What did you do as work? How did you live?

Herdsman
Most of my life was spent among the flocks.   1125

Oedipus
In what part of the country did you live?

Herdsman
Cithaeron and the places near to it.

Oedipus
And somewhere there perhaps you knew this man?

Herdsman
What was his occupation? Who?

Oedipus
> This man here,   1130
have you had any dealings with him?

Herdsman
>   No—
not such that I can quickly call to mind.

Messenger
That is no wonder, master. But I'll make him remember
what he does not know. For I know, that he well knows
the country of Cithaeron, how he with two flocks, I with   1135
one kept company for three years—each year half a year
—from spring till autumn time and then when winter
came I drove my flocks to our fold home again and he
to Laius' steadings. Well—am I right or not in what I   1140
said we did?

Herdsman
You're right—although it's a long time ago.

Messenger
Do you remember giving me a child
to bring up as my foster child?

Herdsman
>   What's this?
Why do you ask this question?

Messenger
>   Look old man,   1145
here he is—here's the man who was that child!

Herdsman
Death take you! Won't you hold your tongue?

Oedipus
>   No, no,
do not find fault with him, old man. Your words
are more at fault than his.

Herdsman
>   O best of masters,
> how do I give offense?

Oedipus
>   When you refuse   1150
> to speak about the child of whom he asks you.

Herdsman
> He speaks out of his ignorance, without meaning.

Oedipus
> If you'll not talk to gratify me, you
> will talk with pain to urge you.

Herdsman
>   O please, sir,
> don't hurt an old man, sir.

Oedipus   (*to the servants.*)
>   Here, one of you,
> twist his hands behind him.

Herdsman
>   Why, God help me, why?   1155
> What do you want to know?

Oedipus
>   You gave a child
> to him,—the child he asked you of?

Herdsman
>   I did.
> I wish I'd died the day I did.

Oedipus

You will
unless you tell me truly.

Herdsman

And I'll die
far worse if I should tell you.

Oedipus

This fellow   1160
is bent on more delays, as it would seem.

Herdsman

O no, no! I have told you that I gave it.

Oedipus

Where did you get this child from? Was it your own or
did you get it from another?

Herdsman

Not
my own at all; I had it from some one.

Oedipus

One of these citizens? or from what house?

Herdsman

O master, please—I beg you, master, please   1165
don't ask me more.

Oedipus

You're a dead man if I
ask you again.

Herdsman

It was one of the children
of Laius.

Oedipus
> A slave? Or born in wedlock?

Herdsman
O God, I am on the brink of frightful speech.

Oedipus
And I of frightful hearing. But I must hear.   1170

Herdsman
The child was called his child; but she within,
your wife would tell you best how all this was.

Oedipus
She gave it to you?

Herdsman
> Yes, she did, my lord.

Oedipus
To do what with it?

Herdsman
> Make away with it.

Oedipus
She was so hard—its mother?   1175

Herdsman
> Aye, through fear
of evil oracles.

Oedipus
> Which?

Herdsman
> They said that he
should kill his parents.

75

Oedipus

How was it that you
gave it away to this old man?

Herdsman

O master,
I pitied it, and thought that I could send it
off to another country and this man
was from another country. But he saved it   1180
for the most terrible troubles. If you are
the man he says you are, you're bred to misery.

Oedipus

O, O, O, they will all come,
all come out clearly! Light of the sun, let me
look upon you no more after today!
I who first saw the light bred of a match
accursed, and accursed in my living
with them I lived with, cursed in my killing.   1185

(*Exeunt all but the Chorus.*)

Chorus

Strophe
O generations of men, how I
count you as equal with those who live
not at all!
What man, what man on earth wins more   1190
of happiness than a seeming
and after that turning away?
Oedipus, you are my pattern of this,
Oedipus, you and your fate!
Luckless Oedipus, whom of all men
I envy not at all.   1196

Antistrophe
In as much as he shot his bolt
beyond the others and won the prize
of happiness complete—
O Zeus—and killed and reduced to nought
the hooked taloned maid of the riddling speech,
standing a tower against death for my land:
hence he was called my king and hence
was honoured the highest of all
honours; and hence he ruled
in the great city of Thebes.

Strophe
But now whose tale is more miserable?   1204
Who is there lives with a savager fate?
Whose troubles so reverse his life as his?

O Oedipus, the famous prince
for whom a great haven
the same both as father and son
sufficed for generation,
how, O how, have the furrows ploughed
by your father endured to bear you, poor wretch,
and hold their peace so long?

Antistrophe
Time who sees all has found you out   1213
against your will; judges your marriage accursed,
begetter and begot at one in it.

O child of Laius,
would I had never seen you.
I weep for you and cry
a dirge of lamentation.

77

To speak directly, I drew my breath
from you at the first and so now I lull   1222
my mouth to sleep with your name.

(*Enter a second Messenger.*)

Second Messenger
O Princes always honoured by our country,
what deeds you'll hear of and what horrors see,
what grief you'll feel, if you as true born Thebans   1225
care for the house of Labdacus's sons.
Phasis nor Ister cannot purge this house,
I think, with all their streams, such things
it hides, such evils shortly will bring forth
into the light, whether they will or not;   1230
and troubles hurt the most
when they prove self-inflicted.

Chorus
What we had known before did not fall short
of bitter groaning's worth; what's more to tell?

Second Messenger
Shortest to hear and tell—our glorious queen   1235
Jocasta's dead.

Chorus
                              Unhappy woman! How?

Second Messenger
By her own hand. The worst of what was done
you cannot know. You did not see the sight.
Yet in so far as I remember it
you'll hear the end of our unlucky queen.   1240
When she came raging into the house she went
straight to her marriage bed, tearing her hair

with both her hands, and crying upon Laius   1245
long dead—Do you remember, Laius,
that night long past which bred a child for us
to send you to your death and leave
a mother making children with her son?
And then she groaned and cursed the bed in which
she brought forth husband by her husband, children   1250
by her own child, an infamous double bond.
How after that she died I do not know,—
for Oedipus distracted us from seeing.
He burst upon us shouting and we looked
to him as he paced frantically around,
begging us always: Give me a sword, I say,   1255
to find this wife no wife, this mother's womb,
this field of double sowing whence I sprang
and where I sowed my children! As he raved
some god showed him the way—none of us there.
Bellowing terribly and led by some   1260
invisible guide he rushed on the two doors,—
wrenching the hollow bolts out of their sockets,
he charged inside. There, there, we saw his wife
hanging, the twisted rope around her neck.
When he saw her, he cried out fearfully   1265
and cut the dangling noose. Then, as she lay,
poor woman, on the ground, what happened after,
was terrible to see. He tore the brooches—
the gold chased brooches fastening her robe—
away from her and lifting them up high
dashed them on his own eyeballs, shrieking out   1270
such things as: they will never see the crime
I have committed or had done upon me!
Dark eyes, now in the days to come look on
forbidden faces, do not recognize
those whom you long for—with such imprecations
he struck his eyes again and yet again   1275
with the brooches. And the bleeding eyeballs gushed

and stained his beard—no sluggish oozing drops
but a black rain and bloody hail poured down.

So it has broken—and not on one head   1280
but troubles mixed for husband and for wife.
The fortune of the days gone by was true
good fortune—but today groans and destruction
and death and shame—of all ills can be named   1285
not one is missing.

Chorus

Is he now in any ease from pain?

Second Messenger

             He shouts
for some one to unbar the doors and show him
to all the men of Thebes, his father's killer,
his mother's—no I cannot say the word,
it is unholy—for he'll cast himself,
out of the land, he says, and not remain   1290
to bring a curse upon his house, the curse
he called upon it in his proclamation. But
he wants for strength, aye, and some one to guide him;
his sickness is too great to bear. You, too,
will be shown that. The bolts are opening.   1295
Soon you will see a sight to waken pity
even in the horror of it.

               (Enter the blinded Oedipus.)

Chorus

This is a terrible sight for men to see!
I never found a worse!
Poor wretch, what madness came upon you!   1300
What evil spirit leaped upon your life

to your ill-luck—a leap beyond man's strength!
Indeed I pity you, but I cannot
look at you, though there's much I want to ask
and much to learn and much to see.   1305
I shudder at the sight of you.

Oedipus
O, O,
where am I going? Where is my voice   1310
borne on the wind to and fro?
Spirit, how far have you sprung?

Chorus
To a terrible place whereof men's ears
may not hear, nor their eyes behold it.

Oedipus
Darkness!
Horror of darkness enfolding, resistless, unspeakable vis-
    itant sped by an ill wind in haste!   1315
madness and stabbing pain and memory
of evil deeds I have done!

Chorus
In such misfortunes it's no wonder
if double weighs the burden of your grief.   1320

Oedipus
My friend,
you are the only one steadfast, the only one that attends
    on me;
you still stay nursing the blind man.
Your care is not unnoticed. I can know   1325
your voice, although this darkness is my world.

Chorus

Doer of dreadful deeds, how did you dare
so far to do despite to your own eyes?
what spirit urged you to it?

Oedipus

It was Apollo, friends, Apollo,
that brought this bitter bitterness, my sorrows to com- 1330
pletion.
But the hand that struck me
was none but my own.
Why should I see
whose vision showed me nothing sweet to see? 1335

Chorus

These things are as you say.

Oedipus

What can I see to love?
What greeting can touch my ears with joy?
Take me away, and haste—to a place out of the way! 1340
Take me away, my friends, the greatly miserable,
the most accursed, whom God too hates 1345
above all men on earth!

Chorus

Unhappy in your mind and your misfortune,
would I had never known you!

Oedipus

Curse on the man who took
the cruel bonds from off my legs, as I lay in the field. 1350
He stole me from death and saved me,
no kindly service.
Had I died then
I would not be so burdensome to friends. 1355

Chorus
  I, too, could have wished it had been so.

Oedipus
  Then I would not have come
  to kill my father and marry my mother infamously.
  Now I am godless and child of impurity,   1360
  begetter in the same seed that created my wretched self.
  If there is any ill worse than ill,   1365
  that is the lot of Oedipus.

Chorus
  I cannot say your remedy was good;
  you would be better dead than blind and living.

Oedipus
  What I have done here was best done—don't tell me   1370
  otherwise, do not give me further counsel.
  I do not know with what eyes I could look
  upon my father when I die and go
  under the earth, nor yet my wretched mother—
  those two to whom I have done things deserving
  worse punishment than hanging. Would the sight   1375
  of children, bred as mine are, gladden me?
  No, not these eyes, never. And my city,
  its towers and sacred places of the Gods,
  of these I robbed my miserable self   1380
  when I commanded all to drive *him* out,
  the criminal since proved by God impure
  and of the race of Laius.
  To this guilt I bore witness against myself—
  with what eyes shall I look upon my people?   1385
  No. If there were a means to choke the fountain
  of hearing I would not have stayed my hand
  from locking up my miserable carcase,
  seeing and hearing nothing; it is sweet   1390
  to keep our thoughts out of the range of hurt.

Cithaeron, why did you receive me? why
having received me did you not kill me straight?
And so I had not shown to men my birth.

O Polybus and Corinth and the house,
the old house that I used to call my father's—   1395
what fairness you were nurse to, and what foulness
festered beneath! Now I am found to be
a sinner and a son of sinners. Crossroads,
and hidden glade, oak and the narrow way
at the crossroads, that drank my father's blood   1400
offered you by my hands, do you remember
still what I did as you looked on, and what
I did when I came here? O marriage, marriage!
you bred me and again when you had bred
bred children of your child and showed to men   1405
brides, wives and mothers and the foulest deeds
that can be in this world of ours.

Come—it's unfit to say what is unfit
to do.—I beg of you in God's name hide me   1410
somewhere outside your country, yes, or kill me,
or throw me into the sea, to be forever
out of your sight. Approach and deign to touch me
for all my wretchedness, and do not fear.
No man but I can bear my evil doom.   1415

Chorus
  Here Creon comes in fit time to perform
  or give advice in what you ask of us.
  Creon is left sole ruler in your stead.

Oedipus
  Creon! Creon! What shall I say to him?
  How can I justly hope that he will trust me?   1420

84

In what is past I have been proved towards him
an utter liar.

(Enter Creon.)

Creon

Oedipus, I've come
not so that I might laugh at you nor taunt you
with evil of the past. But if you still
are without shame before the face of men
reverence at least the flame that gives all life,   1425
our Lord the Sun, and do not show unveiled
to him pollution such that neither land
nor holy rain nor light of day can welcome.

(To a servant.)

Be quick and take him in. It is most decent   1430
that only kin should see and hear the troubles
of kin.

Oedipus

I beg you, since you've torn me from
my dreadful expectations and have come
in a most noble spirit to a man
that has used you vilely—do a thing for me.
I shall speak for your own good, not for my own.

Creon

What do you need that you would ask of me?   1435

Oedipus

Drive me from here with all the speed you can
to where I may not hear a human voice.

Creon

Be sure, I would have done this had not I
wished first of all to learn from the God the course
of action I should follow.

85

Oedipus

But his word   **1440**
has been quite clear to let the parricide,
the sinner, die.

Creon

Yes, that indeed was said.
But in the present need we had best discover
what we should do.

Oedipus

And will you ask about
a man so wretched?

Creon

Now even you will trust **1445**
the God.

Oedipus

So. I command you—
and will beseech you—
to her that lies inside that house give burial
as you would have it; she is yours and rightly
you will perform the rites for her. For me—
never let this my father's city have me **1450**
living a dweller in it. Leave me live
in the mountains where Cithaeron is, that's called
my mountain, which my mother and my father
while they were living would have made my tomb.
So I may die by their decree who sought
indeed to kill me. Yet I know this much: **1455**
no sickness and no other thing will kill me.
I would not have been saved from death if not
for some strange evil fate. Well, let my fate
go where it will.

Creon, you need not care **1460**

86

about my sons; they're men and so wherever
they are, they will not lack a livelihood.
But my two girls—so sad and pitiful—
whose table never stood apart from mine,
and everything I touched they always shared—   1465
O Creon, have a thought for them! And most
I wish that you might suffer me to touch them
and sorrow with them.

> (*Enter Antigone and Ismene,*
> *Oedipus' two daughters.*)

O my lord! O true noble Creon! Can I   1470
really be touching them, as when I saw?
What shall I say?
Yes, I can hear them sobbing—my two darlings!
and Creon has had pity and has sent me
what I loved most?
Am I right?   1475

Creon

You're right: it was I gave you this
because I knew from old days how you loved them
as I see now.

Oedipus

God bless you for it, Creon,
and may God guard you better on your road
than he did me!
O children,   1480
where are you? Come here, come to my hands,
a brother's hands which turned your father's eyes,
those bright eyes you knew once, to what you see,
a father seeing nothing, knowing nothing,
begetting you from his own source of life.   1485
I weep for you—I cannot see your faces—
I weep when I think of the bitterness

87

there will be in your lives, how you must live
before the world. At what assemblages
of citizens will you make one? to what   1490
gay company will you go and not come home
in tears instead of sharing in the holiday?
And when you're ripe for marriage, who will he be,
the man who'll risk to take such infamy
as shall cling to my children, to bring hurt   1495
on them and those that marry with them? What
curse is not there? "Your father killed his father
and sowed the seed where he had sprung himself
and begot you out of the womb that held him."
These insults you will hear. Then who will marry you?   1500
No one, my children; clearly you are doomed
to waste away in barrenness unmarried.
Son of Menoeceus, since you are all the father
left these two girls, and we, their parents, both   1505
are dead to them—do not allow them wander
like beggars, poor and husbandless.
They are of your own blood.
And do not make them equal with myself
in wretchedness; for you can see them now
so young, so utterly alone, save for you only.
Touch my hand, noble Creon, and say yes.   1510
If you were older, children, and were wiser,
there's much advice I'd give you. But as it is,
let this be what you pray: give me a life
wherever there is opportunity
to live, and better life than was my father's.

Creon

  Your tears have had enough of scope; now go within 1515
    the house.

Oedipus

  I must obey, though bitter of heart.

88

Creon
In season, all is good.

Oedipus
Do you know on what conditions I obey?

Creon
You tell me them,
and I shall know them when I hear.

Oedipus
That you shall send me out
to live away from Thebes.

Creon
That gift you must ask of the God

Oedipus
But I'm now hated by the Gods.

Creon
So quickly you'll obtain your prayer.

Oedipus
You consent then?   1520

Creon
What I do not mean,
I do not use to say.

Oedipus
Now lead me away from here.

Creon
Let go the children, then, and come.

Oedipus
Do not take them from me.

Creon
Do not seek to be master in everything,
for the things you mastered did not follow you through-
out your life.

(*As Creon and Oedipus go out.*)

Chorus
You that live in my ancestral Thebes, behold this
Oedipus,—
him who knew the famous riddles and was a man most 1525
masterful;
not a citizen who did not look with envy on his lot—
see him now and see the breakers of misfortune swallow
him!
Look upon that last day always. Count no mortal happy
till
he has passed the final limit of his life secure from pain. 1530

OEDIPUS AT COLONUS

Translated by

ROBERT FITZGERALD

TO THE MEMORY OF MILMAN PARRY

"Nous vivons éternellement, non dans les écoles de pointilleurs de syllabes, mais dans le cercle des sages où l'on ne discute pas sur la mère d'Andromaque ou les fils de Niobé, mais où l'on s'entretient des origines profondes des choses divines et humaines."

CHARACTERS

Oedipus

Antigone

A Stranger

Ismene

Theseus

Creon

Polyneices

A Messenger

The Chorus

ΘEDIPUS AT COLONUS

SCENE: *In the background is the grove of the Furies at Colonus in Attica, about a mile northwest of Athens. A statue or stele of Colonus, a legendary horseman and hero, can be seen stage left. Stage right, a flat rock jutting out among the trees of the grove. Downstage, center, another ridge of rock. Oedipus, old, blind, bearded and ragged, enters, led by Antigone.*

Oedipus
My daughter—daughter of the blind old man—
Where have we come to now, Antigonê?
What lands are these, or holdings of what city?
Who will be kind to Oedipus this evening
And give alms to the wanderer?

Though he ask little and receive still less,   5
It is sufficient:
          Suffering and time,
Vast time, have been instructors in contentment,
Which kingliness teaches too.
          But now, child,
If you can see a resting place—perhaps
A roadside fountain, or some holy grove,   10
Tell me, and let me pause there and sit down;
So we may learn our whereabouts, and take
Our cue from what we hear, as strangers should.

Antigone
 Father, poor tired Oedipus, the towers
 That crown the city still seem far away;
 As for this place, it is clearly a holy one,
 Shady with vines and olive trees and laurel;—
 A covert for the song and hush of nightingales
 In their snug wings.
                     But rest on this rough stone.
 It was a long road for an old man to travel.   20

Oedipus
 Help me sit down; take care of the blind man.

Antigone
 After so long, you need not tell me, father.

Oedipus
 What can you say, now, as to where we are?

Antigone
 This place I do not know; I know the city
 Must be Athens.

Oedipus
                As all the travellers said.   2

Antigone
 Then shall I go and ask what place this is?

Oedipus
 Do, child, if there is any life near-by.

Antigone
 Oh, but indeed there is; I need not leave you;
 I see a man, now, not far away from us.

Oedipus
Is he coming this way? Has he started toward us?   30

(*The Stranger enters, left.*)

Antigone
Here he is now.
               Say what seems best to you,
Father; the man is here.

Oedipus
Friend, my daughter's eyes serve for my own.
She tells me we are fortunate enough to meet you,
And no doubt you will inform us—   35

Stranger
            Do not go on;
First move from where you sit; the place is holy;
It is forbidden to walk upon that ground.

Oedipus
What ground is this? What god is honored here?

Stranger
It is not to be touched, no one may live upon it;
Most dreadful are its divinities, most feared,
Daughters of darkness and mysterious earth.   40

Oedipus
Under what solemn name shall I invoke them?

Stranger
The people here prefer to address them as Gentle
All-seeing Ones; elsewhere there are other names.

Oedipus
Then may they be gentle to the suppliant.
For I shall never leave this resting place.   45

Stranger
What is the meaning of this?

Oedipus
                    It was ordained;
I recognize it now.

Stranger
                    Without authority
From the city government I dare not move you;
First I must show them what you are doing.

Oedipus
Friend, in the name of God, bear with me now!
I turn to you for light; answer the wanderer.   5

Stranger
Speak. You will have no discourtesy from me.

Oedipus
What is this region that we two have entered?

Stranger
As much as I can tell you, I will tell.
This country, all of it, is blessed ground;
The god Poseidon loves it; in it the firecarrier   5
Prometheus has his influence; in particular
That spot you rest on has been called this earth's
Doorsill of Brass, and buttress of great Athens.
All men of this land claim descent from him
Who is sculptured here: Colonus, master horseman,
And bear his name in common with their own.   6

That is this country, stranger: honored less
In histories than in the hearts of the people.

Oedipus
Then people live here on their lands?

Stranger
          They do,
The clan of those descended from that hero.   65

Oedipus
Ruled by a prince, or by the greater number?

Stranger
The land is governed from Athens, by the king.

Oedipus
And who is he whose word has power here?

Stranger
Theseus, son of Aegeus, the king before him.

Oedipus
Ah. Would someone then go to this king for me?   70

Stranger
To tell him what? Perhaps to urge his coming?

Oedipus
To tell him a small favor will gain him much.

Stranger
What service can a blind man render him?

Oedipus
All I shall say will be clear-sighted indeed.

Stranger

Friend, listen to me: I wish you no injury;　　　　　75
You seem well-born, though obviously unlucky;
Stay where you are, exactly where I found you,
And I'll inform the people of what you say—
Not in the town, but here—it rests with them
To decide if you should stay or must move on.　　　80

(Exit Stranger, left.)

Oedipus

Child, has he gone?

Antigone

Yes, father. Now you may speak tranquilly,
For only I am with you.

Oedipus　　　　　　　　　　　　　　*(Praying.)*

Ladies whose eyes
Are terrible: Spirits: upon your sacred ground
I have first bent my knees in this new land;　　　85
Therefore be mindful of me and of Apollo,
For when he gave me oracles of evil,
He also spoke of this:

A resting place,
After long years, in the last country, where
I should find home among the sacred Furies:　　　90
That I might round out there my bitter life.
Conferring benefit on those who received me,
A curse on those who have driven me away.

Portents, he said, would make me sure of this:
Earthquake, thunder, or God's smiling lightning;　　　95
But I am sure of it now, sure that you guided me
With feathery certainty upon this road,
And led me here into your hallowed wood.

How otherwise could I, in my wandering,
Have sat down first with you in all this land,   100
I who drink not, with you who love not wine?

How otherwise had I found this chair of stone?
Grant me then, goddesses, passage from life at last,
And consummation, as the unearthly voice foretold;
Unless indeed I seem not worth your grace: 105
Slave as I am to such unending pain
As no man had before.
                    O hear my prayer,
Sweet children of original Darkness! Hear me,
Athens, city named for great Athena,
Honored above all cities in the world!
Pity a man's poor carcase and his ghost,
For Oedipus is not the strength he was.   110

Antigone
  Be still. Some old, old men are coming this way,
  Looking for the place where you are seated.

Oedipus
  I shall be still. Take me clear of the path,
  And hide me in the wood, so I may hear
  What they are saying. If we know their temper   115
  We shall be better able to act with prudence.

        (*Oedipus and Antigone withdraw into the grove.*
                    The Chorus enters.)

Chorus
  Look for him. Who could he be? Where
  Is he? Where is the stranger
  Impious, blasphemous, shameless!   120
  Use your eyes, search him out!

99

Cover the ground and uncover him!
  Vagabond!
The old man must be a vagabond,
Not of our land, for he'd never   125
Otherwise dare to go in there,
In the inviolate thicket
Of those whom it's futile to fight,
Those whom we tremble to name.
When we pass we avert our eyes—
  Close our eyes!—   130
In silence, without conversation,
Shaping our prayers with our lips
But now, if the story is credible,
Some alien fool has profaned it;
Yet I have looked over all the grove and   135
  Still cannot see him;
Cannot say where he has hidden.

(Oedipus comes forward from the wood.)

Oedipus
  That stranger is I. As they say of the blind,
  Sounds are the things I see.

Chorus
              Ah!   140
  His face is dreadful! His voice is dreadful!

Oedipus
  I beg you not to think me a criminal.

Chorus
  Zeus defend us, who is this old man?

Oedipus
  One whose fate is not quite to be envied,
  O my masters, and men of this land;   145

That must be evident: why, otherwise,
   Should I need this girl
To lead me, her frailty to put my weight on?

Chorus
  Ah! His eyes are blind!   150
  And were you brought into the world so?
  Unhappy life—and so long!
  Well, not if I can stop it,
  Will you have this curse as well.—   155
    Stranger! you
  Trespass there! But beyond there,
  In the glade where the grass is still,
  Where the honeyed libations drip
  In the rill from the brimming spring,
  You must not step! O stranger,   160
  It is well to be careful about it!
    Most careful!
  Stand aside and come down then!
  There is too much space between us!
  Say, wanderer, can you hear?   165
  If you have a mind to tell us
  Your business, or wish to converse with our council,
    Come down from that place!
  Only speak where it's proper to do so!

Oedipus
  Now, daughter, what is the way of wisdom?   170

Antigone
  We must do just as they do here, father;
  We should give in now, and listen to them.

Oedipus
  Stretch out your hand to me.

Antigone

> There, I am near you.

Oedipus

Sirs, let there be no injustice done me,
Once I have trusted you, and left my refuge.   175

(Led by Antigone, he starts downstage.)

Chorus

Never, never, will anyone drive you away
From rest in this land, old man!

Oedipus

Shall I come farther?

Chorus

> Yes, farther.

Oedipus

And now?

Chorus

> You must guide him, girl;   180
You can see how far to come.

Antigone

Come with your blind step, father;
This way; come where I lead you.

Chorus

Stranger in a strange country,
Courage, afflicted man!   185
Whatever the state abhors
You, too, abhor; and honor
Whatever the state holds dear.

Oedipus
  Lead me on, then, child,
  To where we may speak or listen respectfully;   190
  Let us not fight necessity.

Chorus
  Now! Go no farther than that platform there,
  Formed of the natural rock.

Oedipus
  This?

Chorus
            Far enough; you can hear us.

Oedipus
  Shall I sit down?

Chorus
            Yes, sit there   195
  To the left on the ridge of the rock.

Antigone
  Father, this is where I can help you;
  You must keep step with me; gently now.

Oedipus
  Ah, me!

Antigone
  Lean your old body on my arm;   200
  It is I, who love you; let yourself down.

Oedipus
  How bitter blindness is!

(He is seated on the rock downstage, center.)

Chorus
  Now that you are at rest, poor man,
  Tell us, what is your name?
  Who are you, wanderer?   205
  What is the land of your ancestors?

Oedipus
  I am an exile, friends; but do not ask me . . .

Chorus
  What is it you fear to say, old man?

Oedipus
  No, no, no! Do not go on   210
  Questioning me! Do not ask my name!

Chorus
  Why not?

Oedipus

                    My star was unspeakable.

Chorus

                    Speak!

Oedipus
  My child, what can I say to them?

Chorus
  Answer us, stranger; what is your race,
  Who was your father?   215

Oedipus
  God help me, what will become of me, child?

Antigone
  Tell them; there is no other way.

Oedipus
  Well, then, I will; I cannot hide it.

Chorus
  Between you, you greatly delay. Speak up!

Oedipus
  Have you heard of Laius' family?

Chorus
                    Ah!   220

Oedipus
  Of the race of Labdacidae?

Chorus
                    Ah, Zeus!

Oedipus
  And ruined Oedipus?

Chorus
                    You are he!

Oedipus
  Do not take fright from what I say—

Chorus
  Oh, dreadful!

Oedipus
                    I am accursed.

Chorus
                    Oh, fearful!

Oedipus
  Antigonê, what will happen now?   225

Chorus
 Away with you! Out with you! Leave our country!

Oedipus
 And what of the promises you made me?

Chorus
 God will not punish the man
 Who makes return for an injury:
 Deceivers may be deceived: 230
 They play a game that ends
 In grief, and not in pleasure.
 Leave this grove at once!
 Our country is not for you!
 Wind no further   235
 Your clinging evil upon us!

Antigone
 O men of reverent mind!
 Since you will not suffer my father,
 Old man though he is,
 And though you know his story—
 He never knew what he did—   240
 Take pity still on my unhappiness,
 And let me intercede with you for him.
 Not with lost eyes, but looking in your eyes
 As if I were a child of yours, I beg   245
 Mercy for him, the beaten man! O hear me!
 We are thrown upon your mercy as on God's;
    Be kinder than you seem!
 By all you have and own that is dear to you:
 Children, wives, possessions, gods, I pray you!   250
 For you will never see in all the world
    A man whom God has led
    Escape his destiny!

Chorus
　Child of Oedipus, indeed we pity you,
　Just as we pity him for his misfortune;　　　　　　255
　But we tremble to think of what the gods may do;
　We dare not speak more generously!

Oedipus
　What use is reputation then? What good
　Comes of a noble name? A noble fiction!
　For Athens, so they say, excels in piety;　　　　　260
　Has power to save the wretched of other lands;
　Can give them refuge; is unique in this.
　Yet, when it comes to me, where is her refuge?
　You pluck me from these rocks and cast me out,
　All for fear of a name!
　　　　　　　　Or do you dread　　　　　265
　My strength? my actions? I think not, for I
　Suffered those deeds more than I acted them,
　As I might show if it were fitting here
　To tell my father's and my mother's story
　For which you fear me, as I know too well.

　And yet, how was I evil in myself?　　　　　　270
　I had been wronged, I retaliated; even had I
　Known what I was doing, was that evil?
　Then, knowing nothing, I went on. Went on.
　But those who wronged me knew, and ruined me.

　Therefore I beg of you before the gods,　　　　　275
　For the same cause that made you move me—
　In reverence of your gods—give me this shelter,
　And thus accord those powers what is theirs.
　Think: their eyes are fixed upon the just,
　Fixed on the unjust, too; no impious man　　　　280
　Can twist away from them forever.
　Now, in their presence, do not blot your city's

Luster by bending to unholy action;
As you would receive an honest petitioner,
Give me, too, sanctuary; though my face   285
Be dreadful in its look, yet honor me!

For I come here as one endowed with grace
By those who are over Nature; and I bring
Advantage to this race, as you may learn
More fully when some lord of yours is here.   290
Meanwhile be careful to be just.

Chorus

                              Old man,
This argument of yours compels our wonder.
It was not feebly worded. I am content
That higher authorities should judge this matter.   295

Oedipus
And where is he who rules the land, strangers?

Chorus
In his father's city; but the messenger
Who sent us here has gone to fetch him also.

Oedipus
Do you think a blind man will so interest him
As to bring him such a distance?   300

Chorus
I do, indeed, when he has heard your name.

Oedipus
But who will tell him that?

Chorus
It is a long road, and the rumors of travellers
Have a way of wandering. He will have word of them;

Take heart—he will be here. Old man, your name   305
Has gone over all the earth; though he may be
At rest when the news comes, he will come quickly.

Oedipus
Then may he come with luck for his own city,
As well as for me . . . The good befriend themselves.

Antigone
O Zeus! What shall I say? How interpret this?   310

Oedipus
Antigonê, my dear child, what is it?

Antigone
               A woman
Riding a Sicilian pony and coming toward us;
She is wearing a wide Thessalian sun-hat;
I don't know!   315
Is it or isn't it? Or am I dreaming?
I think so; yes!—No. I can't be sure. . . .

Ah, poor child,
It is no one else but she! And she is smiling   320
Now as she comes! It is my dear Ismenê!

Oedipus
What did you say, child?

               (*Ismene enters, with one Attendant.*)

Antigone
             That I see your daughter!
My sister! Now you can tell her by her voice.

Ismene
  O father and sister together! Dearest voices!
  Now I have found you—how, I scarcely know—   325
  I don't know how I shall see you through my tears!

Oedipus
  Child, have you come?

Ismene
              Father, how old you seem!

Oedipus
  Child, are you here?

Ismene
              And such a time I had!

Oedipus
  Touch me, little one.

Ismene
              I shall hold you both!

Oedipus
  My children . . . and sisters.

Ismene
              Oh, unhappy people!   330

Oedipus
  She and I?

Ismene
  And I with you, unhappy.

Oedipus
  Why have you come, child?

Ismene

Thinking of you, father.

Oedipus
You were lonely?

Ismene

Yes; and I bring news for you.
I came with the one person I could trust.

Oedipus
Why, where are your brothers? Could they not do it?   335

Ismene
They are—where they are. It is a hard time for them.

Oedipus
Ah! They behave as if they were Egyptians,
Bred the Egyptian way! Down there, the men
Sit indoors all day long, weaving;
The women go out and attend to business.   340
Just so your brothers, who should have done this work
Sit by the fire like home-loving girls,
And you two, in their place, must bear my hardships.

One, since her childhood ended and her body
Gained its power, has wandered ever with me,   345
An old man's governess; often in the wild
Forest going without shoes, and hungry,
Beaten by many rains, tired by the sun;   350
Yet she rejected the sweet life of home
So that her father should have sustenance.

And you, my daughter, once before came out,
Unknown to Thebes, bringing me news of all
The oracle had said concerning me;   355

And you remained my faithful outpost there,
When I was driven from that land.

But now,
What news, Ismenê, do you bring your father?
Why have you left your house to make this journey?
You came for no light reason, I know that;
It must be something serious for me.   360

Ismene
I will pass over the troubles I have had
Searching for your whereabouts, father.
They were hard enough to bear; and I will not
Go through it all again in telling of them.
In any case, it is your sons' troubles   365
That I have come to tell you.
First it was their desire, as it was Creon's,
That the throne should pass to him; that thus the city
Should be defiled no longer: such was their reasoning
When they considered our people's ancient curse
And how it enthralled your pitiful family.   370
But then some fury put it in their hearts—
O pitiful again!—to itch for power:
For seizure of prerogative and throne;
And it was the younger and the less mature
Who stripped his elder brother, Polyneicês,   375
Of place and kingship, and then banished him.

But now the people hear he has gone to Argos,
Into the valley land, has joined that nation,
And is enlisting friends among its warriors,
Telling them Argos shall honorably win   380
Thebes and her plain, or else eternal glory.
This is not a mere recital, father;
But terrible truth!

How long will it be, I wonder,
Before the gods take pity on your distress?

Oedipus
You have some hope then that they are concerned   385
With my deliverance?

Ismene
                    I have, father.
The latest sentences of the oracle . . .

Oedipus
How are they worded? What do they prophesy?

Ismene
That you shall be much solicited by our people
Before your death—and after—for their welfare.   390

Oedipus
And what could anyone hope from such as I?

Ismene
The oracles declare their strength's in you—

Oedipus
When I am worn to nothing, strength in me?

Ismene
For the gods who threw you down sustain you now.

Oedipus
Slight favor, now I am old! My doom was early.   395

Ismene
The proof of it is that Creon is coming to you
For that same reason, and soon: not by and by.

Oedipus
To do what, daughter? Tell me about this.

Ismene
To settle you near the land of Thebes, and so
Have you at hand; but you may not cross the border.   400

Oedipus
What good am I to Thebes outside the country?

Ismene
It is merely that if your burial were unlucky,
That would be perilous for them.

Oedipus
                              Ah, then!
This does not need divine interpretation.

Ismene
Therefore they want to keep you somewhere near,
Just at the border, where you'll not be free.   405

Oedipus
And will they compose my shade with Theban dust?

Ismene
Ah, father! No. Your father's blood forbids it.

Oedipus
Then they shall never hold me in their power!

Ismene
If not, some day it will be bitter for them.

Oedipus
How will that be, my child?

114

Ismene
When they shall stand   410
Where you are buried, and feel your anger there.

Oedipus
This that you say—from whom did you hear it, child?

Ismene
The envoys told me when they returned from Delphi.

Oedipus
Then all this about me was spoken there?

Ismene
According to those men, just come to Thebes.   415

Oedipus
Has either of my sons had word of this?

Ismene
They both have, and they understand it well.

Oedipus
The scoundrels! So they knew all this, and yet
Would not give up the throne to have me back?

Ismene
It hurts me to hear it, but I can't deny it.   420

Oedipus
Gods!
Never quench their fires of ambition!
Let the last word be mine upon this battle
They are about to join, with the spears lifting!
I'd see that he who holds the sceptre now   425
Would not have power long, nor would the other,
The banished one, return!

These were the two
Who saw me in disgrace and banishment
And never lifted a hand for me. They heard me
Howled from the country, heard the thing proclaimed!   430

And will they say I wanted exile then,
An appropriate clemency, granted by the state?
That is all false! The truth is that at first
My mind was a boiling caldron; nothing so sweet
As death, death by stoning, could have been given me;   435
Yet no one there would grant me that desire.
It was only later, when my madness cooled,
And I had begun to think my rage excessive,
My punishment too great for what I had done;
Then it was that the city—in its good time!—   440
Decided to be harsh, and drove me out.
They could have helped me then; they could have
Helped him who begot them! Would they do it?
For lack of a little word from that fine pair
Out I went, like a beggar, to wander forever!   445
Only by grace of these two girls, unaided,
Have I got food or shelter or devotion;
The others held their father of less worth
Than sitting on a throne and being king.

Well, they shall never win me in their fight!   450
Nor will they profit from the rule of Thebes.
I am sure of that; I have heard the prophecies
Brought by this girl; I think they fit those others
Spoken so long ago, and now fulfilled.
So let Creon be sent to find me: Creon,   455
Or any other of influence in the state.
If you men here consent—as do those powers
Holy and awful, the spirits of this place—
To give me refuge, then shall this city have
A great savior; and woe to my enemies!   460

Chorus
  Oedipus: you are surely worth our pity:
  You, and your children, too. And since you claim
  Also to be a savior of our land,
  I'd like to give you counsel for good luck.

Oedipus
  Dear friend! I'll do whatever you advise.   465

Chorus
  Make expiation to these divinities
  Whose ground you violated when you came.

Oedipus
  In what way shall I do so? Tell me, friends.

Chorus
  First you must bring libations from the spring
  That runs forever; and bring them with clean hands.   470

Oedipus
  And when I have that holy water, then?

Chorus
  There are some bowls there, by a skillful potter;
  Put chaplets round the brims, over the handles.

Oedipus
  Of myrtle sprigs, or woolen stuff? Of what?

Chorus
  Take the fleeces cropped from a young lamb.   475

Oedipus
  Just so; then how must I perform the rite?

Chorus

  Facing the quarter of the morning light,
  Pour your libations out.

Oedipus

  Am I to pour them from the bowls you speak of?

Chorus

  In three streams, yes; the last one, empty it.

Oedipus

  With what should it be filled? Tell me this, too.   480

Chorus

  With water and honey; but with no wine added.

Oedipus

  And when the leaf-dark earth receives it?

Chorus

  Lay three times nine young shoots of olive on it
  With both your hands; meanwhile repeat this prayer:

Oedipus

  I am eager to hear this, for it has great power.   485

Chorus

  That as we call them Eumenidês,
  Which means the gentle of heart,
  May they accept with gentleness
  The suppliant and his wish.

So you, or he who prays for you, address them;

But do not speak aloud or raise a cry;
Then come away, and do not turn again.   490

If you will do all this, I shall take heart
And stand up for you; otherwise, O stranger,
I should be seriously afraid for you.

Oedipus
Children, you hear the words of these good people?

Antigone
Yes; now tell us what we ought to do.

Oedipus
It need not be performed by me; I'm far   495
From having strength or sight for it—I have neither.
Let one of you go and carry out the ritual.
One soul, I think, often can make atonement
For many others, if it be devoted.
Now do it quickly.—Yet do not leave me alone!   500
I could not move without the help of someone.

Ismene
I'll go and do it. But where am I to go?
Where shall I find the holy place, I wonder?

Chorus
On the far side of the wood, girl. If you need it,   505
You may get help from the attendant there.

Ismene
I am going now. Antigonê, you will stay
And care for father. If it were difficult,
I should not think it so, since it is for him.

(*Ismene goes out, right. The Chorus draws
nearer to Oedipus.*)

Chorus
  What evil things have slept since long ago   510
  It is not sweet to waken;
  And yet I long to be told—

Oedipus
                    What?

Chorus
  Of that heartbreak for which there was no help,
      The pain you have had to suffer.

Oedipus
      For kindness' sake, do not open   515
      My old wound, and my shame.

Chorus
  It is told everywhere, and never dies;
  I only want to hear it truly told.

Oedipus
  Ah! Ah!

Chorus
                    Consent I beg you;
  Give me my wish, and I shall give you yours.   520

Oedipus
  I had to face a thing most terrible,
      Not willed by me, I swear;
      I would have abhorred it all.

Chorus
                    So?

Oedipus
  Though I did not know, Thebes married me to evil;   525
      Fate and I were joined there.

Chorus
Then it was indeed your mother
With whom the thing was done?

Oedipus
Ah! It is worse than death to have to hear it!
Strangers! Yes: and these two girls of mine . . .   530

Chorus
You say—?

Oedipus
                    These luckless two
Were given birth by her who gave birth to me.

Chorus
These then are daughters; they are also—

Oedipus
Sisters: yes, their father's sisters . . .   535

Chorus
Ah, pity!

Oedipus
                    Pity, indeed. What throngs
Of pities come into my mind!

Chorus
You suffered—

Oedipus
                    Yes, unspeakably.

Chorus
You sinned—

Oedipus

No, I did not sin!

Chorus

How not?

Oedipus

I thought
Of her as my reward. Ah, would that I had never won it! 540
Would that I had never served the State that day!

Chorus

Unhappy man—and you also killed—

Oedipus

What is it now? What are you after?

Chorus

Killed your father!

Oedipus

God in heaven!
You strike again where I am hurt.

Chorus

You killed him.

Oedipus

Killed him. Yet there is— 545

Chorus

What more?

Oedipus

A just extenuation.
This:

122

I did not know him; and he wished to murder me.
Before the law—before God—I am innocent!

(*The Chorus turns at the approach of Theseus.*)

Chorus
  The king is coming! Aegeus' eldest son,
  Theseus: news of you has brought him here.   550

(*Theseus enters with Soldiers, left.*)

Theseus
  In the old time I often heard men tell
  Of the bloody extinction of your eyes.
  Even if on my way I were not informed,
  I'd recognize you, son of Laius.
  The garments and the tortured face   555
  Make plain your identity. I am sorry for you.
  And I should like to know what favor here
  You hope for from the city and from me:
  Both you and your unfortunate companion.
  Tell me. It would be something dire indeed   560
  To make me leave you comfortless; for I
  Too was an exile. I grew up abroad,
  And in strange lands I fought as few men have
  With danger and with death.
  Therefore no wanderer shall come, as you do,   565
  And be denied my audience or aid.
  I know I am only a man; I have no more
  To hope for in the end than you have.

Oedipus
  Theseus, in those few words your nobility
  Is plain to me. I need not speak at length;   570
  You have named me and my father accurately,
  Spoken with knowledge of my land and exile.

123

There is, then, nothing left for me to tell
But my desire; and then the tale is ended.

Theseus
Tell me your wish, then; let me hear it now.   575

Oedipus
I come to give you something, and the gift
Is my own beaten self: no feast for the eyes;
Yet in me is a more lasting grace than beauty.

Theseus
What grace is this you say you bring to us?

Oedipus
In time you'll learn, but not immediately.   580

Theseus
How long, then, must we wait to be enlightened?

Oedipus
Until I am dead, and you have buried me.

Theseus
Your wish is burial? What of your life meanwhile?
Have you forgotten that?—or do you care?

Oedipus
It is all implicated in my burial.   585

Theseus
But this is a brief favor you ask of me.

Oedipus
See to it, nevertheless! It is not simple.

Theseus
You mean I shall have trouble with your sons?

Oedipus
Those people want to take me back there now.

Theseus
Will you not go? Is exile admirable?   590

Oedipus
No. When I wished to go, they would not have it.

Theseus
What childishness! You are surely in no position—

Oedipus
When you know me, admonish me; not now!

Theseus
Instruct me, then. I must not speak in ignorance.

Oedipus
Theseus, I have been wounded more than once.   595

Theseus
Is it your family's curse that you refer to?

Oedipus
Not merely that; all Hellas talks of that.

Theseus
Then what is the wound that is so pitiless?

Oedipus
Think how it is with me. I was expelled
From my own land by my own sons; and now,   600
As a parricide, my return is not allowed.

Theseus
How can they summon you, if this is so?

Oedipus
The sacred oracle compels them to.

Theseus
They fear some punishment from his forebodings?

Oedipus
They fear they will be struck down in this land!   605

Theseus
And how could war arise between these nations?

Oedipus
Most gentle son of Aegeus! The immortal
Gods alone have neither age nor death!
All other things almighty Time disquiets.
Earth wastes away; the body wastes away;   610
Faith dies; distrust is born.
And imperceptibly the spirit changes
Between a man and his friend, or between two cities.
For some men soon, for others in later time,
Their pleasure sickens; or love comes again.   615
And so with you and Thebes: the sweet season
Holds between you now; but times goes on,
Unmeasured Time, fathering numberless
Nights, unnumbered days: and on one day
They'll break apart with spears this harmony—   620
All for a trivial word.
And then my sleeping and long-hidden corpse,
Cold in the earth, will drink hot blood of theirs,
If Zeus endures; if his son's word is true.

However: there's no felicity in speaking
Of hidden things. Let me come back to this: 625
Be careful that you keep your word to me;
For if you do you'll never say of Oedipus
That he was given refuge uselessly—
Or if you say it, then the gods have lied.

Chorus
    My lord: before you came this man gave promise
    Of having power to make his words come true.   630

Theseus
    Who would reject his friendship? Is he not
    One who would have, in any case, an ally's
    Right to our hospitality?
    Moreover he has asked grace of our deities,
    And offers no small favor in return.   635
    As I value this favor, I shall not refuse
    This man's desire; I declare him a citizen.

    And if it should please our friend to remain here,
    I direct you to take care of him;
    Or else he may come with me.
                            Whatever you choose,
    Oedipus, we shall be happy to accord.   640
    You know your own needs best; I accede to them.

Oedipus
    May God bless men like these!

Theseus
    What do you say then? Shall it be my house?

Oedipus
    If it were right for me. But the place is here . . .

Theseus
And what will you do here?—Not that I oppose you.   64?

Oedipus
Here I shall prevail over those who banished me.

Theseus
Your presence, as you say, is a great blessing.

Oedipus
If you are firm in doing what you promise.

Theseus
You can be sure of me; I'll not betray you.

Oedipus
I'll not ask pledges, as I would of scoundrels.   65o

Theseus
You'd get no more assurance than by my word.

Oedipus
I wonder how you will behave?

Theseus
                        You fear?

Oedipus
That men will come—

Theseus
                        These men will attend to them.

Oedipus
Look: when you leave me—

Theseus

        I know what to do!

Oedipus

I am oppressed by fear!

Theseus

        I feel no fear.   655

Oedipus

You do not know the menace!

Theseus

        I do know
No man is going to take you against my will.
Angry men are liberal with threats
And bluster generally. When the mind
Is master of itself, threats are no matter.
These people may have dared to talk quite fiercely   660
Of taking you; perhaps, as I rather think,
They'll find a sea of troubles in the way.
Therefore I should advise you to take heart.
Even aside from me and my intentions,
Did not Apollo send and guide you here?   665
However it may be, I can assure you,
While I'm away, my name will be your shield.

       (*Exit Theseus and Soldiers. The Chorus
          turns to the audience.*)

Chorus

The land of running horses, fair
Colonus takes a guest;
He shall not seek another home,   670
For this, in all the earth and air,
Is most secure and loveliest.

In the god's untrodden vale
Where leaves and berries throng,
And wine-dark ivy climbs the bough,
The sweet, sojourning nightingale
Murmurs all night long.   675

No sun nor wind may enter there
Nor the winter's rain;
But ever through the shadow goes
Dionysus reveler,
Immortal maenads in his train.   680

Here with drops of heaven's dews
At daybreak all the year,
The clusters of narcissus bloom,
Time-hallowed garlands for the brows
Of those great ladies whom we fear.   685

The crocus like a little sun
Blooms with its yellow ray;
The river's fountains are awake,
And his nomadic streams that run
Unthinned forever, and never stay;   690

But like perpetual lovers move
On the maternal land.
And here the choiring Muses come,
And the divinity of love
With gold reins in her hand.

> (*The Chorus may now shift its grouping
> or otherwise indicate a change of theme.*)

Chorus
   And our land has a thing unknown
   On Asia's sounding coast   695

Or in the sea-surrounded west
Where Pelop's kin hold sway:
The olive, fertile and self-sown,
The terror of our enemies
That no hand tames or tears away—
The blessed tree that never dies!—
But it will mock the swordsman in his rage.

Ah, how it flourishes in every field,
Most beautifully here!   700
The grey-leafed tree, the children's nourisher!
No young man nor one partnered by his age
Knows how to root it out nor make
Barren its yield;
For Zeus Protector of the Shoot has sage
Eyes that forever are awake,   705
And Pallas watches with her sea-grey eyes.
Last and grandest praise I sing
To Athens, nurse of men,
For her great pride and for the splendor
Destiny has conferred on her.   710
Land from which fine horses spring!
Land where foals are beautiful!
Land of the sea and the sea-farer,
Enthroned on her pure littoral
By Cronus' briny son in ancient time.

That lord, Poseidon, must I praise again,
Who found our horsemen fit
For first bestowal of the curb and bit,   715
To discipline the stallion in his prime;
And strokes to which our oarsmen sing,
Well-fitted, oak and men,
Whose long sea-oars in wondrous rhyme
Flash from the salt foam, following
The track of winds on waters virginal.

*(At the conclusion of this, Antigone is standing
stage right, looking off-stage attentively.)*

Antigone
Land so well spoken of and praised so much!   720
Now is the time to show those words are true.

Oedipus
What now, my child?

Antigone   *(Returning to him.)*
                        A man is coming toward us,
And it is Creon—not alone, though, father.

Oedipus
Most kindly friends! I hope you may give proof,
And soon, of your ability to protect me!   725

Chorus
No fear; it will be proved. I may be old
But the nation's strength has not grown old.

                        (Enter Creon, right, with Guards.)
Creon
Gentlemen, and citizens of this land:
I can see from your eyes that my arrival
Has been a cause of sudden fear to you;   730
Do not be fearful. And say nothing hostile!
I have not come for any hostile action,
For I am old, and know this city has
Power, if any city in Hellas has.

But for this man here: I, despite my age,   735
Am sent to bring him to the land of Thebes.

Not one man's mission, this, but it was ordered
By the whole Theban people. I am their emissary
Because it fell to me as a relative
To mourn his troubles more than anyone.

So, now, poor Oedipus, come home.   740
You know the word I bring. Your countrymen
Are right in summoning you—I most of all,
For most of all, unless I am worst of men,
I grieve for your unhappiness, old man.
I see you ravaged as you are, a stranger   745
Everywhere, never at rest,
With only a girl to serve you in your need.—
I never thought she'd fall to such indignity,
Poor child! And yet she has;   750
Forever tending you, leading a beggar's
Life with you; a grown-up girl who knows
Nothing of marriage; whoever comes can take her.

Is this not a disgrace? I weep to see it!
Disgrace for you, for me, for all our people!
We cannot hide what is so palpable,   755
But you, if you will listen to me, Oedipus—
And in the name of your father's gods, listen!—
Bury the whole thing now; agree with me
To go back to your city and your home!

Take friendly leave of Athens, as she merits;
But you should have more reverence for Thebes,
Since long ago she was your kindly nurse.   760

Oedipus
You brazen rascal! Playing your rascal's tricks
In righteous speeches, as you always would!

Why do you try it? How can you think to take me
Into that snare I should so hate if taken?

That time when I was sick with my own life's   765
Evil: when I would gladly have left the earth—
You had no mind to give me what I wanted!
But when at long last I had had my fill
Of rage and grief, and in my quiet house
Began to find some comfort: that was the time
You chose to rout me out.   770
How precious was this kinship then?
It is the same thing now: you see this city
And all its people being kind to me,
So you would draw me away—
A cruel thing, for all your soothing words.

Why is it your pleasure is to be amiable   775
To those who do not want your amiability?
Suppose that when you begged for something desperately
A man should neither grant it you nor give
Sympathy even; but later when you were glutted
With all your heart's desire, should give it then,
When charity was no charity at all?
Would you not think the kindness somewhat hollow?   780
That is the sort of kindness you offer me:
Generous in words, but in reality evil.
Now I will tell these men, and prove you evil.
You come to take me, but not to take me home;
Rather to settle me outside the city
So that the city may escape my curse,   785
Escape from punishment by Athens.
            Yes;
But you'll not have it. What you'll have is this:
My vengeance active in that land forever;
And what my sons will have of my old kingdom
Is just so much room as they need to die in!   790

Now who knows better the destiny of Thebes?
I do, for I have had the best informants:
Apollo, and Zeus himself who is his father.
And yet you come here with your fraudulent speech
All whetted up! The more you talk, the more   795
Harm, not good, you'll get by it!—
However, I know you'll never believe that.—

Only leave us! Let us live here in peace!
Is this misfortune if it brings contentment?

Creon

Which of us do you consider is more injured   800
By talk like this? You hurt only yourself.

Oedipus

I am perfectly content, so long as you
Can neither wheedle me nor fool these others.

Creon

Unhappy man! Shall it be plain that time
Brings you no wisdom? that you shame your age?   805

Oedipus

An agile wit! I know no honest man
Able to speak so well under all conditions!

Creon

To speak much is one thing; to speak to the point another!

Oedipus

As if you spoke so little but so fittingly!

Creon

No, not fittingly for a mind like yours!   810

Oedipus
Leave me! I speak for these men, too!
Spare me your wardship, here where I must live!

Creon
I call on these—not you!—as witnesses
Of what rejoinder you have made to friends.—
If I ever take you—

Oedipus
     With these men opposing,
Who is going to take me by violence?   815

Creon
You'll suffer without need of that, I promise you!

Oedipus
What are you up to? What is behind that brag?

Creon
Your daughters: one of them I have just now
Had seized and carried off; now I'll take this one!

Oedipus
Ah!

Creon
Soon you shall have more reason to groan about it!   820

Oedipus
You have my child?

Creon
     And this one in a moment!

Oedipus
  Ah, friends! What will you do? Will you betray me?
  Expel this man who has profaned your country!

Chorus
  Go, and go quickly, stranger! You have no right
  To do what you are doing, or what you have done!   825

Creon   (*To Guards.*)
  You there: it would be well to take her now,
  Whether she wants to go with you or not.

                  (*Two Guards approach Antigone.*)

Antigone
  Oh, God, where shall I run? What help is there
  From gods or men?

Chorus
                  What are you doing, stranger?

Creon
  I will not touch this man; but she is mine.   830

Oedipus
  O masters of this land!

Chorus
                  This is unjust!

Creon
  No, just!

Chorus
  Why so?

Creon
                  I take what belongs to me!

137

Oedipus
O Athens!

Chorus

What are you doing, strangers? Will you
Let her go? Must we have a test of strength?   835

Creon
Keep off!

Chorus

I will not; you are chargeable!

Creon
Your city will have war if you hurt me!

Oedipus
Did I not proclaim this?

Chorus   (*To Guards.*)
Take your hands
Off the child at once!

Creon

What you cannot enforce,
Do not command!

Chorus
Release the child, I say!

Creon

And I say—March!   840

(*The Guards pull Antigone toward the right.*)

Chorus
  Help! Here, men of Colonus! Help! Help!
  The city, my city, is violated!
  Help, ho!

Antigone
  They drag me away. How wretched! O friends, friends!

Oedipus (*Groping.*)
  Where are you, child?

Antigone
                  They have overpowered me!   845

Oedipus
  Give me your hands, little one!

Antigone
                  I cannot do it!

Creon (*To Guards.*)
  Will you get on with her?

                  (*They go out, right.*)

Oedipus
                  God help me now!

Creon
  With these two sticks at any rate you'll never
  Guide yourself again! But since you wish
  To conquer your own people—by whose command,   850
  Though I am royal, I have performed this act—
  Go on and conquer! Later, I think, you'll learn
  That now as before you have done yourself no good
  By gratifying your temper against your friends!
  Anger has always been your greatest sin!   855

139

Chorus   (*Approaching Creon.*)
  Control yourself, stranger!

Creon
  Don't touch me, I say!

Chorus
  I'll not release you! Those two girls were stolen!

Creon
  By God, I'll have more booty in a moment
  To bring my city! I'll not stop with them!

Chorus
  Now what are you about?

Creon

                    I'll take him, too!   860

Chorus
  A terrible thing to say!

Creon

                    It will be done!

Chorus
  Not if the ruler of our land can help it!

Oedipus
  Voice of shamelessness! Will you touch me?

Creon
  Silence, I say!

Oedipus

                    No! May the powers here
  Not make me silent until I say this curse: 865
  You scoundrel, who have cruelly taken her

Who served my naked eyepits as their eyes!
On you and yours forever may the sun god,
Watcher of all the world, confer such days
As I have had, and such an age as mine!   870

Creon
  Do you see this, men of the Land of Athens?

Oedipus
  They see both me and you; and they see also
  That when I am hurt I have only words to avenge it!

Creon
  I'll not stand for it longer! Alone as I am,
  And slow with age, I'll try my strength to take him!   875

          (Creon goes slowly toward Oedipus.)

Oedipus
  Ah!

Chorus
  You are a bold man, friend,
  If you think you can do this!

Creon
              I do think so!

Chorus
  If you could, our city would be finished!

Creon
  In a just cause the weak will beat the strong!   880

Oedipus
  You hear his talk?

141

Chorus

　　　　　By Zeus, he shall not do it!

Creon

Zeus may determine that, but you will not.

Chorus

Is this not criminal!

Creon　　　　　　　　　(*Laying hold of Oedipus.*)

If so, you'll bear it!

Chorus

Ho, everyone! Captains, ho!
Come on the run!
They are well on their way by now!　　　　885

(*Theseus enters, left, with armed men.*)

Theseus

Why do you shout? What is the matter here?
Of what are you afraid?
You have interrupted me as I was sacrificing
To the great sea god, the patron of Colonus.
Tell me, let me know everything.
I do not care to make such haste for nothing.　　　890

Oedipus

O dearest friend—I recognize your voice—
A fearful thing has just been done to me!

Theseus

What is it? Who is the man who did it? Tell me.

Oedipus

This Creon has had my daughters bound and stolen.　　　895

142

Theseus
  What's this you say?

Oedipus
            Yes; now you know my loss.

Theseus   (*To his men.*)
  One of you go on the double
  To the altar place and rouse the people there;
  Make them leave the sacrifice at once
  And run full speed, both foot and cavalry
  As hard as they can gallop, for the place   900
  Where the two highways come together.
  The girls must not be taken past that point,
  Or I shall be a laughing-stock to this fellow,
  As if I were a man to be handled roughly!
  Go on, do as I tell you! Quick!

                              (*Exit Soldier, left.*)

            This man—
  If I should act in anger, as he deserves,   905
  I would not let him leave my hands unbloodied;
  But he shall be subject to the sort of laws
  He has himself imported here.—

                              (*To Creon.*)
  You: you shall never leave this land of Attica
  Until you produce those girls here in my presence; 910
  For your behavior is an affront to me,
  A shame to your own people and your nation.

  You come to a city-state that practices justice,
  A state that rules by law, and by law only;
  And yet you cast aside her authority,   915
  Take what you please, and worse, by violence,

                              143

As if you thought there were no men among us,
Or only slaves; and as if I were nobody.

I doubt that Thebes is responsible for you:
She has no propensity for breeding rascals.   920
And Thebes would not applaud you if she knew
You tried to trick me and to rob the gods
By dragging helpless people from their sanctuary!

Were I a visitor in your country—
No matter how immaculate my claims—   925
Without consent from him who ruled the land,
Whoever he might be, I should take nothing.
I think I have some notion of the conduct
Proper to one who visits a friendly city.
You bring disgrace upon an honorable
Land—your own land, too; a long life   930
Seems to have left you witless as you are old.

I said it once and say it now again:
Someone had better bring those girls here quickly,
Unless you wish to prolong your stay with us
Under close guard, and not much liking it.   935
This is not just a speech; I mean it, friend.

Chorus
Now do you see where you stand? Thebes is just,
But you are adjudged to have acted wickedly.

Creon
It was not that I thought this state unmanly,
Son of Aegeus; nor ill-governed, either;   940
Rather I did this thing in the opinion
That no one here would love my citizens
So tenderly as to keep them against my will.
And surely, I thought, no one would give welcome

To an unholy man, a parricide,   945
A man with whom his mother had been found!
Such at least was my estimate of the wisdom
Native to the Areopagus; I thought
Athens was not a home for such exiles.
In that belief I considered him my prize.   950
Yet I should not have touched him, had he not
Called down curses on my race and me;
That was an injury that deserved reprisal.
There is no old age for a man's anger,
Only death; the dead cannot be hurt.   955

You will do as you wish in this affair,
For even though my case is right and just,
I am weak, without support. Nevertheless,
Old as I am, I'll try to hold you answerable.

Oedipus

O arrogance unashamed! Whose age do you   960
Think you are insulting, mine or yours?
The bloody deaths, the incest, the calamities
You speak so glibly of: I suffered them,
By fate, against my will! It was God's pleasure,
And perhaps our race had angered him long ago.   965
In me myself you could not find such evil
As would have made me sin against my own.
And tell me this: if there were prophecies
Repeated by the oracles of the gods,
That Father's death should come through his own son,   970
How could you justly blame it upon me?
On me, who was yet unborn, yet unconceived,
Not yet existent for my father and mother?
If then I came into the world—as I did come—
In wretchedness, and met my father in fight,   975
And knocked him down, not knowing that I killed him
Nor whom I killed—again, how could you find

Guilt in that unmeditated act?
As for my mother—damn you, you have no shame,
Though you are her own brother, in forcing me   980
To speak of that unspeakable marriage;
But I shall speak, I'll not be silent now
After you let your foul talk go so far!
Yes, she gave me birth—incredible fate!—
But neither of us knew the truth; and she
Bore my children also—and then her shame.
But one thing I do know: you are content   985
To slander her as well as me for that;
While I would not have married her willingly
Nor willingly would I ever speak of it.

No: I shall not be judged an evil man,
Neither in that marriage nor in that death
Which you forever charge me with so bitterly.—   990
Just answer me one thing:
If someone tried to kill you here and now,
You righteous gentleman, what would you do,
Inquire first if the stranger was your father?
Or would you not first try to defend yourself?
I think that since you like to be alive   995
You'd treat him as the threat required; not
Look around for assurance that you were right.
Well, that was the sort of danger I was in,
Forced into it by the gods. My father's soul,
Were it on earth, I know would bear me out.

You, however, being a knave—and since you   1000
Think it fair to say anything you choose,
And speak of what should not be spoken of—
Accuse me of all this before these people.
You also think it clever to flatter Theseus,
And Athens—her exemplary government;
But in your flattery you have forgotten this: 1005

If any country comprehends the honors
Due to the gods, this country knows them best;
Yet you could steal me from Athens in my age
And in my time of prayer; indeed, you seized me,
And you have seized and carried off my daughters.

Now for that profanation I make my prayer,   1010
Calling on the divinities of the grove
That they shall give me aid and fight for me;
So you may know what men defend this town.

Chorus
My lord, our friend is worthy; he has had
Disastrous fortune; yet he deserves our comfort.   1015

Theseus
Enough of speeches. While the perpetrators
Flee, we who were injured loiter here.

Creon
What will you have me do?—since I am worthless.

Theseus
You lead us on the way. You can be my escort.
If you are holding the children in this neighborhood   1020
You yourself will uncover them to me.
If your retainers have taken them in flight,
The chase is not ours; others are after them.
And they will never have cause to thank their gods
For getting free out of this country.
All right. Move on. And remember that the captor   1025
Is now the captive; the hunter is in the snare.
What was won by stealth will not be kept.

In this you will have no others to assist you;
And I know well you had them, for you'd never

Dare to go so far in your insolence 1030
Were you without sufficient accomplices.
You must have had a reason for your confidence,
And I must reckon with it. The whole city
Must not seem overpowered by one man.
Do you understand at all? Or do you think
That what I say is still without importance? 1035

Creon

To what you say I make no objection here.
At home we, too, shall determine what to do.

Theseus

If you must threaten, do so on the way.
Oedipus, you stay here, and rest assured
That unless I perish first I'll not draw breath 1040
Until I put your children in your hands.

Oedipus

Bless you for your noble heart, Theseus!
And you are blessed in what you do for us!

(Two Soldiers take Creon by the arms and march
him out, right, followed by Theseus and the rest
of his men. The Chorus follows a short way and
stands gazing after them.)

Chorus

Ah, God, to be where the pillagers make stand!
To hear the shout and brazen sound of war! 1045
Or maybe on Apollo's sacred strand,
Or by that torchlit Eleusinian shore

Where pilgrims come, whose lips the golden key 1050
Of sweet-voiced ministers has rendered still,

To cherish there with grave Persephonê
Consummate rest from death and mortal ill;

For even to those shades the warrior king 1055
Will press the fighting on—until he take
The virgin sisters from the foemen's ring,
Within his country, for his country's sake!

It may be they will get beyond the plain
And reach the snowy mountain's western side, 1060
If their light chariots have the racing rein,
If they have ponies, and if they can ride;

Yet they'll be taken: for the god they fear
Fights for our land, and Theseus sends forth 1065
His headlong cavalry with all its gear
Flashing like mountain lightning to the north.

These are the riders of Athens, conquered never;
They honor her whose glory all men know,
And honor the sea god, who is dear forever 1070
To Rhea Mother, who bore him long ago.

*(A shift of grouping, and the following
stanzas taken each by a separate voice.)*

Chorus
Swords out—or has the work of swords begun?
My mind leans to a whisper: 1075
Within the hour they must surrender
The woeful children of the blinded one:
This day is shaped by Zeus Artificer.
I can call up the bright sword play, 1080
But wish the wind would lift me like a dove
Under the tall cloud cover
To look with my own eyes on this affray.

Zeus, lord of all, and eye of heaven on all,   1085
Let our Home Troop's hard riding
Cut them off, and a charge from hiding
Carry the combat in one shock and fall.
Stand, helmeted Athena, at our side.   1090
Apollo, Artemis, come down,
Hunter and huntress of the flickering deer—
Pace with each cavalier
For honor of our land and Athens town.

> (*There is a long pause, and then the
> Chorus turns to Oedipus in joy.*)

Chorus

O wanderer! You will not say I lied;
I who kept lookout for you!
I see them now—the two girls—here they come
With our armed men around them!

Oedipus

What did you say? Ah, where?

> (*Theseus comes in leading by the hand
> Antigone and Ismene, followed by Soldiers.*)

Antigone

O father, father!
I wish some god would give you eyes to see   1100
The noble prince who brings us back to you!

Oedipus

Ah, child! You are really here?

Antigone

Yes, for the might
Of Theseus and his kind followers saved us.

Oedipus
Come to your father, child, and let me touch you
Whom I had thought never to touch again!   1105

Antigone
It shall be as you ask; I wish it as much as you.

Oedipus
Where are you?

Antigone
             We are coming to you together.

Oedipus
My sweet children!

Antigone
            To our father, sweet indeed.

Oedipus
My staff and my support!

Antigone
          And partners in sorrow.

Oedipus
I have what is dearest to me in the world.   1110
To die, now, would not be so terrible,
Since you are near me.
           Press close to me, child,
Be rooted in your father's arms; rest now
From the cruel separation, the going and coming;
And tell me the story as briefly as you can: 1115
A little talk is enough for girls so tired.

151

Antigone

   Theseus saved us: he is the one to tell you;
   And he can put it briefly and make it clear.

Oedipus

   Dear friend: don't be offended if I continue
   To talk to these two children overlong;   1120
   I had scarce thought they would be seen again!
   Be sure I understand that you alone
   Made this joy possible for me.
   You are the one that saved them, no one else.
   And may the gods give you such destiny
   As I desire for you: and for your country.   1125
   For I have found you truly reverent,
   Decent, and straight in speech: you only
   Of all mankind.
   I know it, and I thank you with these words.
   All that I have I owe to your courtesy;—
   Now give me your right hand, my lord,   1130
   And if it be permitted, let me kiss you.

   What am I saying? How can a wretch like me
   Desire to touch a man who has no stain
   Of evil in him? No, no; I will not do it;
   And neither shall you touch me. The only ones   1135
   Fit to be fellow-sufferers of mine
   Are those with such experience as I have.
   Receive my salutation where you are.
   And for the rest, be kindly to me still
   As you have been up to now.

Theseus

   That you should talk a long time to your children
   In joy at seeing them—why, that's no wonder!   1140
   Or that you should address them before me—
   There's no offense in that. It is not in words

That I should wish my life to be distinguished,
But rather in things done.
Have I not shown that? I was not a liar   1145
In what I swore I'd do for you, old man.
I am here; and I have brought them back
Alive and safe, for all they were threatened with.
As to how I found them, how I took them, why
Brag of it? You will surely learn from them.

However, there is a matter that just now   1150
Came to my attention on my way here—
A trivial thing to speak of, and yet puzzling;
I want your opinion on it.
It is best for a man not to neglect such things.

Oedipus
What is it, son of Aegeus? Tell me,
So I may know on what you desire counsel.   1155

Theseus
They say a man has come here claiming to be
A relative of yours, though not of Thebes;
For some reason he has thrown himself in prayer
Before Poseidon's altar, where I was making
Sacrifice before I came.

Oedipus
What is his country? What is he praying for?   1160

Theseus
All I know is this: he asks, they tell me,
A brief interview with you, and nothing more.

Oedipus
Upon what subject?
If he is in prayer, it cannot be a trifle.

153

Theseus

  They say he only asks to speak to you
  And then to depart safely by the same road.   1165

Oedipus

  Who could it be who would come here to pray?

Theseus

  Think: have you any relative in Argos
  Who might desire this favor of you?

Oedipus

                Dear friend!
  Say no more!

Theseus

                What has alarmed you?

Oedipus

  No more!

Theseus

              But: what is the matter? Tell me.   1170

Oedipus

  When I heard "Argos" I knew the petitioner.

Theseus

  And who is he whom I must hold at fault?

Oedipus

  A son of mine, my lord, and a hated one.
  Nothing could be more painful than to listen to him.

Theseus

  But why? Is it not possible to listen   1175
  Without doing anything you need not do?
  Why should it distress you so to hear *him*?

Oedipus
My lord, even his voice is hateful to me.
Don't overrule me; don't make me yield in this!

Theseus
But now consider if you are not obliged
To do so by his supplication here:
Perhaps you have a duty to the god.   1180

Antigone
Father: listen to me, even if I am young.
Allow this man to satisfy his conscience
And give the gods whatever he thinks their due.
And let our brother come here, for my sake.
Don't be afraid: he will not throw you off   1185
In your resolve, nor speak offensively.
What is the harm in hearing what he says?
If he has ill intentions, he'll betray them.
You sired him; even though he wronged you, father,
And wronged you impiously, still you can not   1190
Rightfully wrong him in return!
Do let him come!
                    Other men have bad sons,
And other men are swift to anger: yet
They will accept advice, they will be swayed
By their friends' pleading, even against their nature.
Reflect, not on the present, but on the past;   1195
Think of your mother's and your father's fate
And what you suffered through them! If you do,
I think you'll see how terrible an end
Terrible wrath may have.
You have, I think, a permanent reminder
In your lost, irrecoverable eyes.   1200
Ah, yield to us! If our request is just,
We need not, surely, be importunate;

And you, to whom I have not yet been hard,
Should not be obdurate with me!

Oedipus
    Child, your talk wins you a pleasure
    That will be a pain for me. If you have set   1205
    Your heart on it, so be it.

    Only, Theseus: if he is to come here,
    Let no one have power over my life!

Theseus
    That is the sort of thing I need hear only
    Once, not twice, old man. I do not boast,
    But you should know your life is safe while mine is.   1210

                    (Theseus goes out, left, with his Soldiers,
                    leaving two on guard. The Chorus turns
                    to address the audience.)

Chorus
    Though he has watched a decent age pass by,
    A man will sometimes still desire the world.
    I swear I see no wisdom in that man.
    The endless hours pile up a drift of pain
    More unrelieved each day; and as for pleasure,   1215
    When he is sunken in excessive age,
    You will not see his pleasure anywhere.
    The last attendant is the same for all,
    Old men and young alike, as in its season   1220
    Man's heritage of underworld appears:
    There being then no epithalamion,
    No music and no dance. Death is the finish.

    Not to be born surpasses thought and speech.
    The second best is to have seen the light   1225

156

And then to go back quickly whence we came.
The feathery follies of his youth once over,   1230
What trouble is beyond the range of man?
What heavy burden will he not endure?
Jealousy, faction, quarreling, and battle—
The bloodiness of war, the grief of war.
And in the end he comes to strengthless age,   1235
Abhorred by all men, without company,
Unfriended in that uttermost twilight
Where he must live with every bitter thing.

This is the truth, not for me only,
But for this blind and ruined man.
Think of some shore in the north   1240
Concussive waves make stream
This way and that in the gales of winter:
It is like that with him:
The wild wrack breaking over him
From head to foot, and coming on forever;
Now from the plunging down of the sun,   1245
Now from the sunrise quarter,
Now from where the noonday gleams,
Now from the night and the north.

           (Antigone and Ismene have been looking
           off-stage, left. Antigone turns.)

Antigone

  I think I see the stranger near us now,
  And no man with him, father; but his eyes   1250
  Swollen with weeping as he comes.

                  (Polyneices enters, left.)

Oedipus

          Who comes?

Antigone

    The one whom we have had so long in mind;
    It is he who stands here; it is Polyneicês.

Polyneices

    Ah, now what shall I do? Sisters, shall I
    Weep for my misfortunes or for those   1255
    I see in the old man, my father,
    Whom I have found here in an alien land,
    With two frail girls, an outcast for so long,
    And with such garments! The abominable
    Filth grown old with him, rotting his sides!
    And on his sightless face the ragged hair   1260
    Streams in the wind. There's the same quality
    In the food he carries for his thin old belly.
    All this I learn too late.
    And I swear now that I have been villainous   1265
    In not supporting you! You need not wait
    To hear it said by others!
                    Only, think:
    Compassion limits even the power of God;
    So may there be a limit for you, father!
    For all that has gone wrong may still be healed,
    And surely the worst is passed!   1270

    Why are you silent?
    Speak to me, father! Don't turn away from me!
    Will you not answer me at all? Will you
    Send me away without a word?
                    Not even
    Tell me why you are enraged against me?

    Daughters of Oedipus, my own sisters,   1275
    Try to move your so implacable father;
    Do not let him reject me in such contempt!
    Make him reply!
               I am here on pilgrimage. . . .

Antigone
   Poor brother: you yourself must tell him why.   1280
   As men speak on they may sometimes give pleasure,
   Sometimes annoy, or sometimes touch the heart;
   And so somehow provide the mute with voices.

Polyneices
   I will speak out then; your advice is fair.
   First, however, I must claim the help   1285
   Of that same god, Poseidon, from whose altars
   The governor of this land has lifted me
   And sent me here, giving me leave to speak
   And to await response, and a safe passage.
   These are the favors I desire from you,
   Stranger, and from my sisters and my father.   1290

   And now, father, I will tell you why I came.
   I am a fugitive, driven from my country,
   Because I thought fit, as the eldest born,
   To take my seat upon your sovereign throne.
   For that, Eteoclês, the younger of us,   1295
   Banished me—but not by a decision
   In argument or ability or arms;
   Merely because he won the city over.
   Of this I believe the Furies that pursue you
   Were indeed the cause: and so I hear   1300
   From clairvoyants whom I afterwards consulted.

   Then, when I went into the Dorian land,
   I took Adrastus as my father-in-law,
   And bound to me by oath whatever men
   Were known as leaders or as fighters there;
   My purpose being to form an expedition
   Of seven troops of spearmen against Thebes.—   1305
   With which enlistment may I die for justice
   Or else expel the men who exiled me!

So it is. Then why should I come here now?
Father, my prayers must be made to you!
Mine and those of all who fight with me!   1310
Their seven columns under seven captains
Even now complete the encirclement of Thebes:
Men like Amphiareus, the hard spear thrower,
Expert in spears and in the ways of eagles;
Second is Tydeus, the Aetolian,   1315
Son of Oeneus; third is Eteoclus,
Born in Argos; fourth is Hippomedon
(His father, Talaus, sent him); Capaneus,
The fifth, has sworn he'll raze the town of Thebes
With fire-brands; and sixth is Parthenopaeus,   1320
An Arcadian who roused himself to war—
Son of that virgin famous in the old time
Who long years afterward conceived and bore him—
Parthenopaeus, Atalanta's son.
And it is I, your son—or if I am not
Truly your son, since evil fathered me,
At least I am called your son—it is I who lead
The fearless troops of Argos against Thebes.   1325

Now in the name of these two children, father,
And for your own soul's sake, we all implore
And beg you to give up your heavy wrath
Against me! I go forth to punish him,
The brother who robbed me of my fatherland!   1330
If we can put any trust in oracles,
They say that those you bless shall come to power.

Now by the gods and fountains of our people,
I pray you, listen and comply! Are we not beggars
Both of us, and exiles, you and I?   1335
We live by paying court to other men;
The same fate follows us.
But as for him—how insupportable!—

He lords it in our house, luxuriates there,
Laughs at us both!
If you will stand by me in my resolve,
I'll waste no time or trouble whipping him;   1340
And then I'll re-establish you at home,
And settle there myself, and throw him out.
If your will is the same as mine, it's possible
To promise this. If not, I can't be saved.   1345

Chorus

For the sake of the one who sent him, Oedipus,
Speak to this man before you send him back.

Oedipus

Yes, gentlemen: but were it not Theseus,
The sovereign of your land, who sent him here,   1350
Thinking it right that he should have an answer,
You never would have heard a sound from me.

Well: he has asked, and he shall hear from me
A kind of answer that will not overjoy him.
You scoundrel!
                    When it was you who held
Throne and authority—as your brother now   1355
Holds them in Thebes—you drove me into exile:
Me, your own father: made me a homeless man,
Insuring me these rags you maunder over
When you behold them now—now that you, too,
Have fallen on evil days and are in exile.

Weeping is no good now. However long   1360
My life may last, I have to see it through;
But I regard you as a murderer!
For you reduced me to this misery,
You made me an alien. Because of you

161

I have begged my daily bread from other men.
If I had not these children to sustain me,   1365
I might have lived or died for all your interest.
But they have saved me, they are my support,
And are not girls, but men, in faithfulness.
As for you two, you are no sons of mine!

And so it is that there are eyes that watch you   1370
Even now; though not as they shall watch
If those troops are in fact marching on Thebes.
You cannot take that city. You'll go down
All bloody, and your brother, too.
                         For I
Have placed that curse upon you before this,   1375
And now I invoke that curse to fight for me,
That you may see a reason to respect
Your parents, though your birth was as it was;
And though I am blind, not to dishonor me.
These girls did not.

And so your supplication and your throne   1380
Are overmastered surely,—if accepted
Justice still has a place in the laws of God.
Now go! For I abominate and disown you!
Wretched scum! Go with the malediction
I here pronounce for you: that you shall never   1385
Master your native land by force of arms,
Nor ever see your home again in Argos,
The land below the hills; but you shall die
By your own brother's hand, and you shall kill
The brother who banished you. For this I pray.
And I cry out to the hated underworld   1390
That it may take you home; cry out to those
Powers indwelling here; and to that Power
Of furious War that filled your hearts with hate!

Now you have heard me. Go: tell it to Thebes,
Tell all the Thebans; tell your faithful fighting
Friends what sort of honors   1395
Oedipus has divided between his sons!

Chorus

Polyneicês, I find no matter for sympathy
In your directing yourself here. You may
Retire.

Polyneices

    Ah, what a journey! What a failure!
My poor companions! See the finish now   1400
Of all we marched from Argos for! See me . . .
For I can neither speak of this to anyone
Among my friends, nor lead them back again;
I must go silently to meet this doom.

O sisters—daughters of his, sisters of mine!   1405
You heard the hard curse of our father:
For God's sweet sake, if father's curse comes true,
And if you find some way to return home,
Do not, at least, dishonor me in death!
But give me a grave and what will quiet me.   1410
Then you shall have, besides the praise he now
Gives you for serving him, an equal praise
For offices you shall have paid my ghost.

Antigone

Polyneicês, I beseech you, listen to me!

Polyneices

Dearest—what is it? Tell me, Antigonê.   1415

Antigone

Withdraw your troops to Argos as soon as you can.
Do not go to your own death and your city's!

Polyneices
  But that is impossible. How could I command
  That army, even backward, once I faltered?

Antigone
  Now why, boy, must your anger rise again?   1420
  What is the good of laying waste your homeland?

Polyneices
  It is shameful to run; and it is also shameful
  To be a laughing-stock to a younger brother.

Antigone
  But see how you fulfill his prophecies!
  Did he not cry that you should kill each other?   1425

Polyneices
  He wishes that. But I cannot give way.

Antigone
  Ah, I am desolate! But who will dare
  Go with you, after hearing the prophecies?

Polyneices
  I'll not report this trifle. A good commander
  Tells heartening news, or keeps the news to himself.   1430

Antigone
  Then you have made up your mind to this, my brother?

Polyneices
  Yes. And do not try to hold me back.
  The dark road is before me; I must take it,
  Doomed by my father and his avenging Furies.
  God bless you if you do what I have asked: 1435
  It is only in death that you can help me now.

Now let me go. Good-bye! You will not ever
Look in my eyes again.

Antigone

You break my heart!

Polyneices
Do not grieve for me.

Antigone

Who would not grieve for you,
Sweet brother! You go with open eyes to death!   1440

Polyneices
Death, if that must be.

Antigone

No! Do as I ask!

Polyneices
You ask the impossible.

Antigone

Then I am lost,
If I must be deprived of you!

Polyneices

All that
Rests with the powers that are over us,—
Whether it must be so or otherwise.
You two—I pray no evil comes to you,   1445
For all men know you merit no more pain.

(*Polyneices goes out, left. There is a dead
silence; then the Chorus meditates.*)

Chorus
    So in this new event we see
    New forms of terror working through the blind,
    Or else inscrutable destiny.   1450
    I am not one to say "This is in vain"
    Of anything allotted to mankind.
    Though some must fall, or fall to rise again,
    Time watches all things steadily—   1455

                    (*A terrific peal of thunder.*)

Ah, Zeus! Heaven's height has cracked!

                        (*Thunder and lightning.*)

Oedipus
    O my child, my child! Could someone here—
    Could someone bring the hero, Theseus?

Antigone
    Father, what is your reason for calling him?

Oedipus
    God's beating thunder, any moment now,   1460
    Will clap me underground: send for him quickly!

                        (*Thunder and lightning.*)

Chorus
    Hear it cascading down the air!
    The god-thrown, the gigantic, holy sound!
    Terror crawls to the tips of my hair!   1465
    My heart shakes!
                    There the lightning flames again!

What heavenly marvel is it bringing 'round?
I fear it, for it never comes in vain,
But for man's luck or his despair. . . .   1470

(*Thunder and lightning.*)

Ah, Zeus! Majestic heaven!

Oedipus
My children, the appointed end has come;
I can no longer turn away from it.

Antigone
How do you know? What is the sign that tells you?

Oedipus
I know it clearly now. Let someone quickly   1475
Send for the king and bring him here to me!

(*Thunder and lightning.*)

Chorus
Hear the wild thunder fall!
Towering Nature is transfixed!
Be merciful, great spirit, if you run   1480
This sword of darkness through our mother land;
Come not for our confusion,
And deal no blows to me,
Though your tireless Furies stand
By him whom I have looked upon.
Great Zeus, I make my prayer to thee!   1485

Oedipus
Is the king near by? Will he come in time
To find me still alive, my mind still clear?

167

Antigone
  Tell me what it is you have in mind!

Oedipus
  To give him now, in return for his great kindness,
  The blessing that I promised I would give.   1490

                                          (*Thunder.*)

Chorus
  O noble son, return!
  No matter if you still descend
  In the deep fastness of the sea god's grove,
  To make pure offering at his altar fire:
  Come back quickly, for God's love!   1495
  Receive from this strange man
  Whatever may be his heart's desire
  That you and I and Athens are worthy of.
  My lord, come quickly as you can!

          (*The thunder continues, until it stops abruptly
                    with the entrance of Theseus, left.*)

Theseus
  Now why do you all together   1500
  Set up this shout once more?
  I see it comes from you, as from our friend.
  Is it a lightning bolt from Zeus? a squall
  Of rattling hail? Those are familiar things
  When such a tempest rages over heaven.

Oedipus
  My lord, I longed for you to come! This is   1505
  God's work, your lucky coming.

Theseus
>Now, what new
Circumstance has arisen, son of Laius?

Oedipus
My life sinks in the scale: I would not die
Without fulfilling what I promised Athens.

Theseus
What proof have you that your hour has come?   1510

Oedipus
The great, incessant thunder and continuous
Flashes of lightning from the hand of Zeus.   1515

Theseus
I believe you. I have seen you prophesy
Many things, none falsely. What must be done?

Oedipus
I shall disclose to you, O son of Aegeus,
What is appointed for you and for your city:
A thing that age will never wear away.
Presently now, without a soul to guide me,   1520
I'll lead you to the place where I must die;
But you must never tell it to any man,
Not even the neighborhood in which it lies.
If you obey, this will count more for you
Than many shields and many neighbors' spears.   1525
These things are mysteries, not to be explained;
But you will understand when you come there
Alone. Alone, because I cannot disclose it
To any of your men or to my children,
Much as I love and cherish them. But you
Keep it secret always, and when you come   1530
To the end of life, then you must hand it on

169

To your most cherished son, and he in turn
Must teach it to his heir, and so forever.
That way you shall forever hold this city
Safe from the men of Thebes, the dragon's sons.

For every nation that lives peaceably,
There will be many others to grow hard
And push their arrogance to extremes: the gods   1535
Attend to these things slowly. But they attend
To those who put off God and turn to madness!
You have no mind for that, child of Aegeus;
Indeed, you know already all that I teach.

Let us proceed then to that place   1540
And hesitate no longer; I am driven
By an insistent voice that comes from God.
Children, follow me this way: see, now
I have become your guide, as you were mine!
Come: do not touch me: let me alone discover
The holy and funereal ground where I   1545
Must take this fated earth to be my shroud.

This way, O come! The angel of the dead,
Hermês, and veiled Persephonê lead me on!

(*He leads them, firmly and slowly, to the left.*)

O sunlight of no light! Once you were mine!
This is the last my flesh will feel of you;   1550
For now I go to shade my ending day
In the dark underworld. Most cherished friend!
I pray that you and this your land and all
Your people may be blessed: remember me,
Be mindful of my death, and be
Fortunate in all the time to come!   1555

*(Oedipus goes out, followed by his chil-
dren and by Theseus with his Soldiers.
The Chorus lifts its arms to pray.)*

Chorus

If I may dare to adore that Lady
The living never see,
And pray to the master of spirits plunged in night,
Who of vast Hell has sovereignty;
Let not our friend go down in grief and weariness   1560
To that all-shrouding cold,
The dead men's plain, the house that has no light.
Because his sufferings were great, unmerited and untold,   1565
Let some just god relieve him from distress!

O powers under the earth, and tameless
Beast in the passage way,   1570
Rumbler prone at the gate of the strange hosts,
Their guard forever, the legends say:
I pray you, even Death, offspring of Earth and Hell,
To let the descent be clear   1575
As Oedipus goes down among the ghosts
On those dim fields of underground that all men living
    fear.
Eternal sleep, let Oedipus sleep well!

(A long pause. A Messenger comes in, left.)

Messenger

Citizens, the briefest way to tell you
Would be to say that Oedipus is no more;   1580
But what has happened cannot be told so simply—
It was no simple thing.

Chorus

He is gone, poor man?

171

Messenger
  You may be sure that he has left this world.

Chorus
  By God's mercy, was his death a painless one?   1585

Messenger
  That is the thing that seems so marvelous.
  You know, for you were witnesses, how he
  Left this place with no friend leading him,
  Acting, himself, as guide for all of us.
  Well, when he came to the steep place in the road,   1590
  The embankment there, secured with steps of brass,
  He stopped in one of the many branching paths.

  This was not far from the stone bowl that marks
  Theseus' and Pirithous' covenant.

  Half-way between that place of stone
  With its hollow pear tree, and the marble tomb,   1595
  He sat down and undid his filthy garments;
  Then he called his daughters and commanded
  That they should bring him water from a fountain
  For bathing and libation to the dead.
  From there they saw the hillcrest of Demeter,   1600
  Freshener of all things: they ascended it
  And soon came back with water for their father;
  Then helped him properly to bathe and dress.

  When everything was finished to his pleasure,
  And no command of his remained undone,   1605
  Then the earth groaned with thunder from the god below;
  And as they heard the sound, the girls shuddered,
  And dropped to their father's knees, and began wailing,
  Beating their breasts and weeping as if heartbroken.
  And hearing them cry out so bitterly,   1610
  He put his arms around them, and said to them:

"Children, this day your father is gone from you.
All that was mine is gone. You shall no longer
Bear the burden of taking care of me—
I know it was hard, my children.—And yet one word   1615
Frees us of all the weight and pain of life:
That word is love. Never shall you have more
From any man than you have had from me.
And now you must spend the rest of life without me."

That was the way of it. They clung together   1620
And wept, all three. But when they finally stopped,
And no more sobs were heard, then there was
Silence, and in the silence suddenly
A voice cried out to him—of such a kind
It made our hair stand up in panic fear: 1625
Again and again the call came from the god:
"Oedipus! Oedipus! Why are we waiting?
You delay too long; you delay too long to go!"

Then, knowing himself summoned by the spirit,
He asked that the lord Theseus come to him;   1630
And when he had come, said: "O my prince and friend,
Give your right hand now as a binding pledge
To my two daughters; children, give him your hands.
Promise that you will never willingly
Betray them, but will carry out in kindness
Whatever is best for them in the days to come."   1635

And Theseus swore to do it for his friend,
With such restraint as fits a noble king.
And when he had done so, Oedipus at once
Laid his blind hands upon his daughters, saying:
"Children, you must show your nobility,   1640
And have the courage now to leave this spot.
You must not wish to see what is forbidden,
Or hear what may not afterward be told.

But go—go quickly. Only the lord Theseus
May stay to see the thing that now begins."

This much every one of us heard him say,   1645
And then we came away with the sobbing girls.
But after a little while as we withdrew
We turned around—and nowhere saw that man,
But only the king, his hands before his face,   1650
Shading his eyes as if from something fearful,
Awesome and unendurable to see.
Then very quickly we saw him do reverence
To Earth and to the powers of the air,
With one address to both.

                But in what manner   1655
Oedipus perished, no one of mortal men
Could tell but Theseus. It was not lightning,
Bearing its fire from Zeus, that took him off;
No hurricane was blowing.   1660
But some attendant from the train of Heaven
Came for him; or else the underworld
Opened in love the unlit door of earth.
For he was taken without lamentation,
Illness or suffering; indeed his end
Was wonderful if mortal's ever was.   1665

Should someone think I speak intemperately,
I make no apology to him who thinks so.

Chorus
But where are his children and the others with them?

Messenger
They are not far away; the sound of weeping
Should tell you now that they are coming here.

(*Antigone and Ismene enter together.*)

174

Antigone
Now we may weep, indeed. 1670
Now, if ever, we may cry
In bitter grief against our fate,
Our heritage still unappeased.
In other days we stood up under it,
Endured it for his sake,
The unrelenting horror. Now the finish 1675
Comes, and we know only
In all that we have seen and done
Bewildering mystery.

Chorus
What happened?

Antigone
We can only guess, my friends.

Chorus
He has gone?

Antigone
He has; as one could wish him to.
Why not? It was not war
Nor the deep sea that overtook him, 1680
But something invisible and strange
Caught him up—or down—
Into a space unseen.
But we are lost. A deathly
Night is ahead of us.
For how, in some far country wandering, 1685
Or on the lifting seas,
Shall we eke out our lives?

Ismene
I cannot guess. But as for me
I wish that charnel Hell would take me 1690

In one death with our father.
This is such desolation
I cannot go on living.

Chorus
  Most admirable sisters:
  Whatever God has brought about
  Is to be borne with courage.
  You must not feed the flames of grief.   1695
  No blame can come to you.

Antigone
  One may long for the past
  Though at the time indeed it seemed
  Nothing but wretchedness and evil.
  Life was not sweet, yet I found it so
  When I could put my arms around my father.
  O father! O my dear!   1700
  Now you are shrouded in eternal darkness,
  Even in that absence
  You shall not lack our love,
  Mine and my sister's love.

Chorus
  He lived his life.

Antigone
                    He did as he had wished!

Chorus
  What do you mean?

Antigone
                    In this land among strangers   1705
  He died where he chose to die.
  He has his eternal bed well shaded,

And in his death is not unmourned.
My eyes are blind with tears
From weeping for you, father.   1710
The terror and the loss
Cannot be quieted.
I know you wished to die in a strange country,
Yet your death was so lonely!
Why could I not be with you?

Ismene
O pity! What is left for me?   1715
What destiny awaits us both
Now we have lost our father?

Chorus
Dear children, remember   1720
That his last hour was free and blessed.
So make an end of grieving!
Is anyone in all the world
Safe from unhappiness?

Antigone
Let us run back there!

Ismene
            Why, what shall we do?

Antigone
I am carried away with longing—

Ismene
            For what,—tell me!   1725

Antigone
To see the resting place in the earth—

Ismene

         Of whom?

Antigone
Father's! O what misery I feel!

Ismene
But that is not permitted. Do you not see?

Antigone
Do not rebuke me!

Ismene

      —And remember, too—   1730

Antigone
Oh, what?

Ismene

          He had no tomb, there was no one
           near!

Antigone
Take me there and you can kill me, too!

Ismene
Ah! I am truly lost!
Helpless and so forsaken!   1735
Where shall I go and how shall I live?

Chorus
You must not fear, now.

Antigone

         Yes, but where is a refuge?

Chorus
A refuge has been found—

Antigone

Where do you mean?

Chorus
A place where you will be unharmed!

Antigone

No . . .   1740

Chorus
What are you thinking?

Antigone

I think there is no way
For me to get home again.

Chorus

Do not go home!

Antigone
My home is in trouble.

Chorus

So it has been before.

Antigone
There was no help for it then: but now it is worse.   1745

Chorus
A wide and desolate world it is for you.

Antigone
Great God! What way is left me?
Do the powers that rule our lives
Still press me on to hope at all?   1750

(*Theseus comes in, with Attendants.*)

179

Theseus
  Mourn no more, children. Those to whom
  The night of earth gives benediction
  Should not be mourned. Retribution comes.

Antigone
  Theseus: we fall on our knees to you.

Theseus
  What is it that you desire, children?   1755

Antigone
  We wish to see the place ourselves
  In which our father rests.

Theseus
                    No, no.
  It is not permissible to go there.

Antigone
  My lord and ruler of Athens, why?

Theseus
  Because your father told me, children,   1760
  That no one should go near the spot,
  No mortal man should tell of it,
  Since it is holy, and is his.
  And if I kept this pledge, he said,
  I should preserve my land from its enemies.   1765
  I swore I would, and the god heard me:
  The oathkeeper who makes note of all.

Antigone
  If this was our father's cherished wish,
  We must be satisfied.
  Send us back, then, to ancient Thebes,   1770

And we may stop the bloody war
From coming between our brothers!

Theseus
  I will do that, and whatever else
  I am able to do for your happiness,
  For his sake who has gone just now   1775
  Beneath the earth. I must not fail.

Chorus
  Now let the weeping cease;
  Let no one mourn again.
  These things are in the hands of God.

ANTIGONE

Translated by

ELIZABETH WYCKOFF

CHARACTERS

Antigone
Ismene
Chorus of Theban Elders
Creon
A Guard
Haemon
Teiresias
A Messenger
Eurydice

ANTIGONE

SCENE: *Thebes, before the royal palace. Antigone and Ismene*
emerge from its great central door.

Antigone
  My sister, my Ismene, do you know
  of any suffering from our father sprung
  that Zeus does not achieve for us survivors?
  There's nothing grievous, nothing free from doom,
  not shameful, not dishonored, I've not seen.
  Your sufferings and mine.
  And now, what of this edict which they say
  the commander has proclaimed to the whole people?
  Have you heard anything? Or don't you know
  that the foes' trouble comes upon our friends?   10

Ismene
  I've heard no word, Antigone, of our friends.
  Not sweet nor bitter, since that single moment
  when we two lost two brothers
  who died on one day by a double blow.
  And since the Argive army went away
  this very night, I have no further news
  of fortune or disaster for myself.

Antigone
  I knew it well, and brought you from the house
  for just this reason, that you alone may hear.

Ismene
  What is it? Clearly some news has clouded you.   20

Antigone
  It has indeed. Creon will give the one
  of our two brothers honor in the tomb;
  the other none.
  Eteocles, with just entreatment treated,
  as law provides he has hidden under earth
  to have full honor with the dead below.
  But Polyneices' corpse who died in pain,
  they say he has proclaimed to the whole town
  that none may bury him and none bewail,
  but leave him unwept, untombed, a rich sweet sight
  for the hungry birds' beholding.   30
  Such orders they say the worthy Creon gives
  to you and me—yes, yes, I say to *me*—
  and that he's coming to proclaim it clear
  to those who know it not.
  Further: he has the matter so at heart
  that anyone who dares attempt the act
  will die by public stoning in the town.
  So there you have it and you soon will show
  if you are noble, or fallen from your descent.

Ismene
  If things have reached this stage, what can I do,
  poor sister, that will help to make or mend?   40

Antigone
  Think will you share my labor and my act.

Ismene
  What will you risk? And where is your intent?

Antigone
  Will you take up that corpse along with me?

Ismene
  To bury him you mean, when it's forbidden?

Antigone
  My brother, and yours, though you may wish he were not.
  I never shall be found to be his traitor.

Ismene
  O hard of mind! When Creon spoke against it!

Antigone
  It's not for him to keep me from my own.

Ismene
  Alas. Remember, sister, how our father
  perished abhorred, ill-famed.   50
  Himself with his own hand, through his own curse
  destroyed both eyes.
  Remember next his mother and his wife
  finishing life in the shame of the twisted strings.
  And third two brothers on a single day,
  poor creatures, murdering, a common doom
  each with his arm accomplished on the other.
  And now look at the two of us alone.
  We'll perish terribly if we force law
  and try to cross the royal vote and power.   60
  We must remember that we two are women
  so not to fight with men.
  And that since we are subject to strong power
  we must hear these orders, or any that may be worse.
  So I shall ask of them beneath the earth
  forgiveness, for in these things I am forced,
  and shall obey the men in power. I know
  that wild and futile action makes no sense.

Antigone

    I wouldn't urge it. And if now you wished
    to act, you wouldn't please me as a partner.   70
    Be what you want to; but that man shall I
    bury. For me, the doer, death is best.
    Friend shall I lie with him, yes friend with friend,
    when I have dared the crime of piety.
    Longer the time in which to please the dead
    than that for those up here.
    There shall I lie forever. You may see fit
    to keep from honor what the gods have honored.

Ismene

    I shall do no dishonor. But to act
    against the citizens. I cannot.

Antigone

    That's your protection. Now I go, to pile   80
    the burial-mound for him, my dearest brother.

Ismene

    Oh my poor sister. How I fear for you!

Antigone

    For me, don't borrow trouble. Clear your fate.

Ismene

    At least give no one warning of this act;
    you keep it hidden, and I'll do the same.

Antigone

    Dear God! Denounce me. I shall hate you more
    if silent, not proclaiming this to all.

Ismene

    You have a hot mind over chilly things.

Antigone

  I know I please those whom I most should please.

Ismene

  If but you can. You crave what can't be done.   90

Antigone

  And so, when strength runs out, I shall give over.

Ismene

  Wrong from the start, to chase what cannot be.

Antigone

  If that's your saying, I shall hate you first,
  and next the dead will hate you in all justice.
  But let me and my own ill-counselling
  suffer this terror. I shall suffer nothing
  as great as dying with a lack of grace.

Ismene

  Go, since you want to. But know this: you go
  senseless indeed, but loved by those who love you.

      (Ismene returns to the palace; Antigone leaves
      by one of the side entrances. The Chorus now
      enters from the other side.)

Chorus

  Sun's own radiance, fairest light ever shone on the gates
    of Thebes,   100
  then did you shine, O golden day's
  eye, coming over Dirce's stream,
  on the Man who had come from Argos with all his armor
  running now in headlong fear as you shook his bridle
    free.

He was stirred by the dubious quarrel of Polyneices. 110
So, screaming shrill,
like an eagle over the land he flew,
covered with white-snow wing,
with many weapons,
with horse-hair crested helms.

He who had stood above our halls, gaping about our
   seven gates,
with that circle of thirsting spears.
Gone, without our blood in his jaws, 120
before the torch took hold on our tower-crown.
Rattle of war at his back; hard the fight for the dragon's
   foe.

The boasts of a proud tongue are for Zeus to hate.
So seeing them streaming on
in insolent clangor of gold, 130
he struck with hurling fire him who rushed
for the high wall's top,
to cry conquest abroad.

Swinging, striking the earth he fell
fire in hand, who in mad attack,
had raged against us with blasts of hate.
He failed. He failed of his aim.
For the rest great Ares dealt his blows about,
first in the war-team. 140

The captains stationed at seven gates
fought with seven and left behind
their brazen arms as an offering
to Zeus who is turner of battle.
All but those wretches, sons of one man,
one mother's sons, who sent their spears

each against each and found the share
of a common death together.

Great-named Victory comes to us
answering Thebe's warrior-joy.
Let us forget the wars just done   150
and visit the shrines of the gods.
All, with night-long dance which Bacchus will lead,
who shakes Thebe's acres.

> (*Creon enters from the palace.*)

Now here he comes, the king of the land,
Creon, Menoeceus' son,
newly named by the gods' new fate.
What plan that beats about his mind
has made him call this council-session,   160
sending his summons to all?

Creon
My friends, the very gods who shook the state
with mighty surge have set it straight again.
So now I sent for you, chosen from all,
first that I knew you constant in respect
to Laius' royal power; and again
when Oedipus had set the state to rights,
and when he perished, you were faithful still
in mind to the descendants of the dead.
When they two perished by a double fate,   170
on one day struck and striking and defiled
each by his own hand, now it comes that I
hold all the power and the royal throne
through close connection with the perished men.
You cannot learn of any man the soul,
the mind, and the intent until he shows
his practise of the government and law.
For I believe that who controls the state

191

and does not hold to the best plans of all,
but locks his tongue up through some kind of fear, 180
that he is worst of all who are or were.
And he who counts another greater friend
than his own fatherland, I put him nowhere.
So I—may Zeus all-seeing always know it—
could not keep silent as disaster crept
upon the town, destroying hope of safety.
Nor could I count the enemy of the land
friend to myself, not I who know so well
that she it is who saves us, sailing straight,
and only so can we have friends at all. 190
With such good rules shall I enlarge our state.
And now I have proclaimed their brother-edict.
In the matter of the sons of Oedipus,
citizens, know: Eteocles who died,
defending this our town with champion spear,
is to be covered in the grave and granted
all holy rites we give the noble dead.
But his brother Polyneices whom I name
the exile who came back and sought to burn 200
his fatherland, the gods who were his kin,
who tried to gorge on blood he shared, and lead
the rest of us as slaves—
it is announced that no one in this town
may give him burial or mourn for him.
Leave him unburied, leave his corpse disgraced,
a dinner for the birds and for the dogs.
Such is my mind. Never shall I, myself,
honor the wicked and reject the just.
The man who is well-minded to the state
from me in death and life shall have his honor. 210

Chorus
This resolution, Creon, is your own,
in the matter of the traitor and the true.

For you can make such rulings as you will
about the living and about the dead.

Creon
Now you be sentinels of the decree.

Chorus
Order some younger man to take this on.

Creon
Already there are watchers of the corpse.

Chorus
What other order would you give us, then?

Creon
Not to take sides with any who disobey.

Chorus
No fool is fool as far as loving death.   220

Creon
Death is the price. But often we have known
men to be ruined by the hope of profit.

(*Enter, from the side, a Guard.*)

Guard
Lord, I can't claim that I am out of breath
from rushing here with light and hasty step,
for I had many haltings in my thought
making me double back upon my road.
My mind kept saying many things to me:
"Why go where you will surely pay the price?"
"Fool, are you halting? And if Creon learns
from someone else, how shall you not be hurt?"   230
Turning this over, on I dilly-dallied.

And so a short trip turns itself to long.
Finally, though, my coming here won out.
If what I say is nothing, still I'll say it.
For I come clutching to one single hope
that I can't suffer what is not my fate.

Creon

What is it that brings on this gloom of yours?

Guard

I want to tell you first about myself.
I didn't do it, didn't see who did it.
It isn't right for me to get in trouble.   240

Creon

Your aim is good. You fence the fact around.
It's clear you have some shocking news to tell.

Guard

Terrible tidings make for long delays.

Creon

Speak out the story, and then get away.

Guard

I'll tell you. Someone left the corpse just now,
burial all accomplished, thirsty dust
strewn on the flesh, the ritual complete.

Creon

What are you saying? What man has dared to do it?

Guard

I wouldn't know. There were no marks of picks,
no grubbed-out earth. The ground was dry and hard,   250

no trace of wheels. The doer left no sign.
When the first fellow on the day-shift showed us,
we all were sick with wonder.
For he was hidden, not inside a tomb,
light dust upon him, enough to turn the curse,
no wild beast's track, nor track of any hound
having been near, nor was the body torn.
We roared bad words about, guard against guard,   260
and came to blows. No one was there to stop us.
Each man had done it, nobody had done it
so as to prove it on him—we couldn't tell.
We were prepared to hold to red-hot iron,
to walk through fire, to swear before the gods
we hadn't done it, hadn't shared the plan,
when it was plotted or when it was done.
And last, when all our sleuthing came out nowhere,
one fellow spoke, who made our heads to droop
low toward the ground. We couldn't disagree.   270
We couldn't see a chance of getting off.
He said we had to tell you all about it.
We couldn't hide the fact.
So he won out. The lot chose poor old me
to win the prize. So here I am unwilling,
quite sure you people hardly want to see me.
Nobody likes the bringer of bad news.

Chorus
Lord, while he spoke, my mind kept on debating.
Isn't this action possibly a god's?

Creon
Stop now, before you fill me up with rage,   280
or you'll prove yourself insane as well as old.
Unbearable, your saying that the gods
take any kindly forethought for this corpse.
Would it be they had hidden him away,

195

honoring his good service, his who came
to burn their pillared temples and their wealth,
even their land, and break apart their laws?
Or have you seen them honor wicked men?
It isn't so.
No, from the first there were some men in town   290
who took the edict hard, and growled against me,
who hid the fact that they were rearing back,
not rightly in the yoke, no way my friends.
These are the people—oh it's clear to me—
who have bribed these men and brought about the deed.
No current custom among men as bad
as silver currency. This destroys the state;
this drives men from their homes; this wicked teacher
drives solid citizens to acts of shame.
It shows men how to practise infamy   300
and know the deeds of all unholiness.
Every least hireling who helped in this
brought about then the sentence he shall have.
But further, as I still revere great Zeus,
understand this, I tell you under oath,
if you don't find the very man whose hands
buried the corpse, bring him for me to see,
not death alone shall be enough for you
till living, hanging, you make clear the crime.
For any future grabbings you'll have learned   310
where to get pay, and that it doesn't pay
to squeeze a profit out of every source.
For you'll have felt that more men come to doom
through dirty profits than are kept by them.

Guard
  May I say something? Or just turn and go?

Creon
  Aren't you aware your speech is most unwelcome?

196

Guard
Does it **annoy your** hearing or your mind?

Creon
Why are you out to allocate my pain?

Guard
The doer hurts your mind. I hurt your ears.

Creon
You are a quibbling rascal through and through.   320

Guard
But anyhow I never did the deed.

Creon
And you the man who sold your mind for money!

Guard
Oh!
How terrible to guess, and guess at lies!

Creon
Go pretty up your guesswork. If you don't
show me the doers you will have to say
that wicked payments work their own revenge.

Guard
Indeed, I pray he's found, but yes or no,
taken or not as luck may settle it,
you won't see me returning to this place.
Saved when I neither hoped nor thought to be,   330
I owe the gods a mighty debt of thanks.

> (*Creon enters the palace. The Guard
> leaves by the way he came.*)

197

Chorus

Many the wonders but nothing walks stranger than man.
This thing crosses the sea in the winter's storm,
making his path through the roaring waves.
And she, the greatest of gods, the earth—
ageless she is, and unwearied—he wears her away
as the ploughs go up and down from year to year   340
and his mules turn up the soil.

Gay nations of birds he snares and leads,
wild beast tribes and the salty brood of the sea,
with the twisted mesh of his nets, this clever man.
He controls with craft the beasts of the open air,
walkers on hills. The horse with his shaggy mane   350
he holds and harnesses, yoked about the neck,
and the strong bull of the mountain.

Language, and thought like the wind
and the feelings that make the town;
he has taught himself, and shelter against the cold,
refuge from rain. He can always help himself.
He faces no future helpless. There's only death
that he cannot find an escape from. He has contrived   360
refuge from illnesses once beyond all cure.

Clever beyond all dreams
the inventive craft that he has
which may drive him one time or another to well or ill.
When he honors the laws of the land and the gods'
    sworn right
high indeed is his city; but stateless the man   370
who dares to dwell with dishonor. Not by my fire,
never to share my thoughts, who does these things.

(*The Guard enters with Antigone.*)

198

My mind is split at this awful sight.
I know her. I cannot deny
Antigone is here.
Alas, the unhappy girl,
her unhappy father's child.   380
Oh what is the meaning of this?
It cannot be you that they bring
for breaking the royal law,
caught in open shame.

Guard

This is the woman who has done the deed.
We caught her at the burying. Where's the king?

(*Creon enters.*)

Chorus

Back from the house again just when he's needed.

Creon

What must I measure up to? What has happened?

Guard

Lord, one should never swear off anything.
Afterthought makes the first resolve a liar.
I could have vowed I wouldn't come back here   390
after your threats, after the storm I faced.
But joy that comes beyond the wildest hope
is bigger than all other pleasure known.
I'm here, though I swore not to be, and bring
this girl. We caught her burying the dead.
This time we didn't need to shake the lots;
mine was the luck, all mine.
So now, lord, take her, you, and question her
and prove her as you will. But I am free.
And I deserve full clearance on this charge.   400

199

Creon
Explain the circumstance of the arrest.

Guard
She was burying the man. You have it all.

Creon
Is this the truth? And do you grasp its meaning?

Guard
I saw her burying the very corpse
you had forbidden. Is this adequate?

Creon
How was she caught and taken in the act?

Guard
It was like this: when we got back again
struck with those dreadful threatenings of yours,
we swept away the dust that hid the corpse.   410
We stripped it back to slimy nakedness.
And then we sat to windward on the hill
so as to dodge the smell.
We poked each other up with growling threats
if anyone was careless of his work.
For some time this went on, till it was noon.
The sun was high and hot. Then from the earth
up rose a dusty whirlwind to the sky,
filling the plain, smearing the forest-leaves,
clogging the upper air. We shut our eyes,   420
sat and endured the plague the gods had sent.
So the storm left us after a long time.
We saw the girl. She cried the sharp and shrill
cry of a bitter bird which sees the nest
bare where the young birds lay.
So this same girl, seeing the body stripped,

cried with great groanings, cried a dreadful curse
upon the people who had done the deed.
Soon in her hands she brought the thirsty dust,
and holding high a pitcher of wrought bronze   430
she poured the three libations for the dead.
We saw this and surged down. We trapped her fast;
and she was calm. We taxed her with the deeds
both past and present. Nothing was denied.
And I was glad, and yet I took it hard.
One's own escape from trouble makes one glad;
but bringing friends to trouble is hard grief.
Still, I care less for all these second thoughts
than for the fact that I myself am safe.   440

Creon
You there, whose head is drooping to the ground,
do you admit this, or deny you did it?

Antigone
I say I did it and I don't deny it.

Creon   (*to the Guard.*)
Take yourself off wherever you wish to go
free of a heavy charge.

Creon   (*to Antigone.*)
You—tell me not at length but in a word.
You knew the order not to do this thing?

Antigone
I knew, of course I knew. The word was plain.

Creon
And still you dared to overstep these laws?

Antigone

For me it was not Zeus who made that order.   450
Nor did that Justice who lives with the gods below
mark out such laws to hold among mankind.
Nor did I think your orders were so strong
that you, a mortal man, could over-run
the gods' unwritten and unfailing laws.
Not now, nor yesterday's, they always live,
and no one knows their origin in time.
So not through fear of any man's proud spirit
would I be likely to neglect these laws,
draw on myself the gods' sure punishment.
I knew that I must die; how could I not?   460
even without your warning. If I die
before my time, I say it is a gain.
Who lives in sorrows many as are mine
how shall he not be glad to gain his death?
And so, for me to meet this fate, no grief.
But if I left that corpse, my mother's son,
dead and unburied I'd have cause to grieve
as now I grieve not.
And if you think my acts are foolishness
the foolishness may be in a fool's eye.   470

Chorus

The girl is bitter. She's her father's child.
She cannot yield to trouble; nor could he.

Creon

These rigid spirits are the first to fall.
The strongest iron, hardened in the fire,
most often ends in scraps and shatterings.
Small curbs bring raging horses back to terms.
Slave to his neighbor, who can think of pride?
This girl was expert in her insolence   480
when she broke bounds beyond established law.

Once she had done it, insolence the second,
to boast her doing, and to laugh in it.
I am no man and she the man instead
if she can have this conquest without pain.
She is my sister's child, but were she child
of closer kin than any at my hearth,
she and her sister should not so escape
their death and doom. I charge Ismene too.
She shared the planning of this burial.   490
Call her outside. I saw her in the house,
maddened, no longer mistress of herself.
The sly intent betrays itself sometimes
before the secret plotters work their wrong.
I hate it too when someone caught in crime
then wants to make it seem a lovely thing.

Antigone
Do you want more than my arrest and death?

Creon
No more than that. For that is all I need.

Antigone
Why are you waiting? Nothing that you say
fits with my thought. I pray it never will.   500
Nor will you ever like to hear my words.
And yet what greater glory could I find
than giving my own brother funeral?
All these would say that they approved my act
did fear not mute them.
(A king is fortunate in many ways,
and most, that he can act and speak at will.)

Creon
None of these others see the case this way.

Antigone
They see, and do not say. You have them cowed.

Creon
And you are not ashamed to think alone?   510

Antigone
No, I am not ashamed. When was it shame
to serve the children of my mother's womb?

Creon
It was not your brother who died against him, then?

Antigone
Full brother, on both sides, my parents' child.

Creon
Your act of grace, in his regard, is crime.

Antigone
The corpse below would never say it was.

Creon
When you honor him and the criminal just alike?

Antigone
It was a brother, not a slave, who died.

Creon
Died to destroy this land the other guarded.

Antigone
Death yearns for equal law for all the dead.

Creon
Not that the good and bad draw equal shares.   520

204

Antigone
  Who knows that this is holiness below?

Creon
  Never the enemy, even in death, a friend.

Antigone
  I cannot share in hatred, but in love.

Creon
  Then go down there, if you must love, and love
  the dead. No woman rules me while I live.

  (*Ismene is brought from the palace under guard.*)

Chorus
  Look there! Ismene is coming out.
  She loves her sister and mourns,
  with clouded brow and bloodied cheeks,
  tears on her lovely face.   530

Creon
  You, lurking like a viper in the house,
  who sucked me dry. I looked the other way
  while twin destruction planned against the throne.
  Now tell me, do you say you shared this deed?
  Or will you swear you didn't even know?

Ismene
  I did the deed, if she agrees I did.
  I am accessory and share the blame.

Antigone
  Justice will not allow this. You did not
  wish for a part, nor did I give you one.

Ismene
You are in trouble, and I'm not ashamed   540
to sail beside you into suffering.

Antigone
Death and the dead, they know whose act it was.
I cannot love a friend whose love is words.

Ismene
Sister, I pray, don't fence me out from honor,
from death with you, and honor done the dead.

Antigone
Don't die along with me, nor make your own
that which you did not do. My death's enough.

Ismene
When you are gone what life can be my friend?

Antigone
Love Creon. He's your kinsman and your care.

Ismene
Why hurt me, when it does yourself no good?   550

Antigone
I also suffer, when I laugh at you.

Ismene
What further service can I do you now?

Antigone
To save yourself. I shall not envy you.

Ismene
Alas for me. Am I outside your fate?

Antigone
Yes. For you chose to live when I chose death.

Ismene
At least I was not silent. You were warned.

Antigone
Some will have thought you wiser. Some will not.

Ismene
And yet the blame is equal for us both.

Antigone
Take heart. You live. My life died long ago.
And that has made me fit to help the dead.   560

Creon
One of these girls has shown her lack of sense
just now. The other had it from her birth.

Ismene
Yes, lord. When people fall in deep distress
their native sense departs, and will not stay.

Creon
You chose your mind's distraction when you chose
to work out wickedness with this wicked girl.

Ismene
What life is there for me to live without her?

Creon
Don't speak of her. For she is here no more.

Ismene
But will you kill your own son's promised bride?

Creon
Oh, there are other furrows for his plough.

Ismene
But where the closeness that has bound these two?   570

Creon
Not for my sons will I choose wicked wives.

Ismene
Dear Haemon, your father robs you of your rights.

Creon
You and your marriage trouble me too much.

Ismene
You will take away his bride from your own son?

Creon
Yes. Death will help me break this marriage off.

Chorus
It seems determined that the girl must die.

Creon
You helped determine it. Now, no delay!
Slaves, take them in. They must be women now.
No more free running.
Even the bold will fly when they see Death   580
drawing in close enough to end their life.

(*Antigone and Ismene are taken inside.*)

Chorus
Fortunate they whose lives have no taste of pain.
For those whose house is shaken by the gods
escape no kind of doom. It extends to all the kin

like the wave that comes when the winds of Thrace
run over the dark of the sea.
The black sand of the bottom is brought from the depth;   590
the beaten capes sound back with a hollow cry.

Ancient the sorrow of Labdacus' house, I know.
Dead men's grief comes back, and falls on grief.
No generation can free the next.
One of the gods will strike. There is no escape.
So now the light goes out
for the house of Oedipus, while the bloody knife   600
cuts the remaining root. Folly and Fury have done this.

What madness of man, O Zeus, can bind your power?
Not sleep can destroy it who ages all,
nor the weariless months the gods have set. Unaged in
     time
monarch you rule of Olympus' gleaming light.   610
Near time, far future, and the past,
one law controls them all:
any greatness in human life brings doom.

Wandering hope brings help to many men.
But others she tricks from their giddy loves,
and her quarry knows nothing until he has walked into
     flame.
Word of wisdom it was when someone said,   620
"The bad becomes the good
to him a god would doom."
Only briefly is that one from under doom.

(Haemon enters from the side.)

Here is your one surviving son.
Does he come in grief at the fate of his bride,
in pain that he's tricked of his wedding?   630

Creon

  Soon we shall know more than a seer could tell us.
  Son, have you heard the vote condemned your bride?
  And are you here, maddened against your father,
  or are we friends, whatever I may do?

Haemon

  My father, I am yours. You keep me straight
  with your good judgment, which I shall ever follow.
  Nor shall a marriage count for more with me
  than your kind leading.

Creon

  There's my good boy. So should you hold at heart
  and stand behind your father all the way.   640
  It is for this men pray they may beget
  households of dutiful obedient sons,
  who share alike in punishing enemies,
  and give due honor to their father's friends.
  Whoever breeds a child that will not help
  what has he sown but trouble for himself,
  and for his enemies laughter full and free?
  Son, do not let your lust mislead your mind,
  all for a woman's sake, for well you know
  how cold the thing he takes into his arms   650
  who has a wicked woman for his wife.
  What deeper wounding than a friend no friend?
  Oh spit her forth forever, as your foe.
  Let the girl marry somebody in Hades.
  Since I have caught her in the open act,
  the only one in town who disobeyed,
  I shall not now proclaim myself a liar,
  but kill her. Let her sing her song of Zeus
  who guards the kindred.
  If I allow disorder in my house

I'd surely have to licence it abroad. 660
A man who deals in fairness with his own,
he can make manifest justice in the state.
But he who crosses law, or forces it,
or hopes to bring the rulers under him,
shall never have a word of praise from me.
The man the state has put in place must have
obedient hearing to his least command
when it is right, and even when it's not.
He who accepts this teaching I can trust,
ruler, or ruled, to function in his place,
to stand his ground even in the storm of spears, 670
a mate to trust in battle at one's side.
There is no greater wrong than disobedience.
This ruins cities, this tears down our homes,
this breaks the battle-front in panic-rout.
If men live decently it is because
discipline saves their very lives for them.
So I must guard the men who yield to order,
not let myself be beaten by a woman.
Better, if it must happen, that a man
should overset me.
I won't be called weaker than womankind. 680

Chorus

We think—unless our age is cheating us—
that what you say is sensible and right.

Haemon

Father, the gods have given men good sense,
the only sure possession that we have.
I couldn't find the words in which to claim
that there was error in your late remarks.
Yet someone else might bring some further light.
Because I am your son I must keep watch

on all men's doing where it touches you,
their speech, and most of all, their discontents.
Your presence frightens any common man   690
from saying things you would not care to hear.
But in dark corners I have heard them say
how the whole town is grieving for this girl,
unjustly doomed, if ever woman was,
to die in shame for glorious action done.
She would not leave her fallen, slaughtered brother
there, as he lay, unburied, for the birds
and hungry dogs to make an end of him.
Isn't her real desert a golden prize?
This is the undercover speech in town.   700
Father, your welfare is my greatest good.
What loveliness in life for any child
outweighs a father's fortune and good fame?
And so a father feels his children's faring.
Then, do not have one mind, and one alone
that only your opinion can be right.
Whoever thinks that he alone is wise,
his eloquence, his mind, above the rest,
come the unfolding, shows his emptiness.
A man, though wise, should never be ashamed   710
of learning more, and must unbend his mind.
Have you not seen the trees beside the torrent,
the ones that bend them saving every leaf,
while the resistant perish root and branch?
And so the ship that will not slacken sail,
the sheet drawn tight, unyielding, overturns.
She ends the voyage with her keel on top.
No, yield your wrath, allow a change of stand.
Young as I am, if I may give advice,
I'd say it would be best if men were born   720
perfect in wisdom, but that failing this
(which often fails) it can be no dishonor
to learn from others when they speak good sense.

Chorus
  Lord, if your son has spoken to the point
  you should take his lesson. He should do the same.
  Both sides have spoken well.

Creon
  At my age I'm to school my mind by his?
  This boy instructor is my master, then?

Haemon
  I urge no wrong. I'm young, but you should watch
  my actions, not my years, to judge of me.

Creon
  A loyal action, to respect disorder?   730

Haemon
  I wouldn't urge respect for wickedness.

Creon
  You don't think she is sick with that disease?

Haemon
  Your fellow-citizens maintain she's not.

Creon
  Is the town to tell me how I ought to rule?

Haemon
  Now there you speak just like a boy yourself.

Creon
  Am I to rule by other mind than mine?

Haemon
  No city is property of a single man.

Creon
But custom gives possession to the ruler.

Haemon
You'd rule a desert beautifully alone.

Creon (*to the Chorus.*)
It seems he's firmly on the woman's side.   740

Haemon
If you're a woman. It is you I care for.

Creon
Wicked, to try conclusions with your father.

Haemon
When you conclude unjustly, so I must.

Creon
Am I unjust, when I respect my office?

Haemon
You tread down the gods' due. Respect is gone.

Creon
Your mind is poisoned. Weaker than a woman!

Haemon
At least you'll never see me yield to shame.

Creon
Your whole long argument is but for her.

Haemon
And you, and me, and for the gods below.

Creon
You shall not marry her while she's alive.   750

Haemon
Then she shall die. Her death will bring another.

Creon
Your boldness has made progress. Threats, indeed!

Haemon
No threat, to speak against your empty plan.

Creon
Past due, sharp lessons for your empty brain.

Haemon
If you weren't father, I should call you mad.

Creon
Don't flatter me with "father," you woman's slave.

Haemon
You wish to speak but never wish to hear.

Creon
You think so? By Olympus, you shall not
revile me with these tauntings and go free.
Bring out the hateful creature; she shall die
full in his sight, close at her bridegroom's side.   760

Haemon
Not at my side her death, and you will not
ever lay eyes upon my face again.
Find other friends to rave with after this.

(Haemon leaves, by one of the side entrances.)

Chorus
  Lord, he has gone with all the speed of rage.
  When such a man is grieved his mind is hard.

Creon
  Oh, let him go, plan superhuman action.
  In any case the girls shall not escape.

Chorus
  You plan for both the punishment of death?   770

Creon
  Not her who did not do it. You are right.

Chorus
  And what death have you chosen for the other?

Creon
  To take her where the foot of man comes not.
  There shall I hide her in a hollowed cave
  living, and leave her just so much to eat
  as clears the city from the guilt of death.
  There, if she prays to Death, the only god
  of her respect, she may manage not to die.
  Or she may learn at last and even then
  how much too much her labor for the dead.   780

                    (*Creon returns to the palace.*)

Chorus
  Love unconquered in fight, love who falls on our havings.
  You rest in the bloom of a girl's unwithered face.
  You cross the sea, you are known in the wildest lairs.
  Not the immortal gods can fly,
  nor men of a day. Who has you within him is mad.   790

You twist the minds of the just. Wrong they pursue and
    are ruined.
You made this quarrel of kindred before us now.
Desire looks clear from the eyes of a lovely bride:
power as strong as the founded world.
For there is the goddess at play with whom no man can   800
    fight.

    (*Antigone is brought from the palace under guard.*)

Now I am carried beyond all bounds.
My tears will not be checked.
I see Antigone depart
to the chamber where all men sleep.

Antigone
Men of my fathers' land, you see me go
my last journey. My last sight of the sun,
then never again. Death who brings all to sleep   810
takes me alive to the shore
of the river underground.
Not for me was the marriage-hymn, nor will anyone start
    the song
at a wedding of mine. Acheron is my mate.

Chorus
With praise as your portion you go
in fame to the vault of the dead.
Untouched by wasting disease,
not paying the price of the sword,   820
of your own motion you go.
Alone among mortals will you descend
in life to the house of Death.

Antigone
Pitiful was the death that stranger died,
our queen once, Tantalus' daughter. The rock

it covered her over, like stubborn ivy it grew.
Still, as she wastes, the rain
and snow companion her.
Pouring down from her mourning eyes comes the water
 that soaks the stone.   830
My own putting to sleep a god has planned like hers.

Chorus

 God's child and god she was.
 We are born to death.
 Yet even in death you will have your fame,
 to have gone like a god to your fate,
 in living and dying alike.

Antigone

 Laughter against me now. In the name of our fathers'
  gods,
 could you not wait till I went? Must affront be thrown in
  my face?   840
 O city of wealthy men.
 I call upon Dirce's spring,
 I call upon Thebe's grove in the armored plain,
 to be my witnesses, how with no friend's mourning,
 by what decree I go to the fresh-made prison-tomb.
 Alive to the place of corpses, an alien still,   850
 never at home with the living nor with the dead.

Chorus

 You went to the furthest verge
 of daring, but there you found
 the high foundation of justice, and fell.
 Perhaps you are paying your father's pain.

Antigone

 You speak of my darkest thought, my pitiful father's
  fame,

spread through all the world, and the doom that haunts
   our house,   860
the royal house of Thebes.
My mother's marriage-bed.
Destruction where she lay with her husband-son,
my father. These are my parents and I their child.
I go to stay with them. My curse is to die unwed.
My brother, you found your fate when you found your   870
   bride,
found it for me as well. Dead, you destroy my life.

Chorus
  You showed respect for the dead.
  So we for you: but power
  is not to be thwarted so.
  Your self-sufficiency has brought you down.

Antigone
  Unwept, no wedding-song, unfriended, now I go
  the road laid down for me.
  No longer shall I see this holy light of the sun.   880
  No friend to bewail my fate.

            (Creon enters from the palace.)

Creon
  When people sing the dirge for their own deaths
  ahead of time, nothing will break them off
  if they can hope that this will buy delay.
  Take her away at once, and open up
  the tomb I spoke of. Leave her there alone.
  There let her choose: death, or a buried life.
  No stain of guilt upon us in this case,
  but she is exiled from our life on earth.   890

Antigone
  O tomb, O marriage-chamber, hollowed out
  house that will watch forever, where I go.

To my own people, who are mostly there;
Persephone has taken them to her.
Last of them all, ill-fated past the rest,
shall I descend, before my course is run.
Still when I get there I may hope to find
I come as a dear friend to my dear father,
to you, my mother, and my brother too.
All three of you have known my hand in death.   900
I washed your bodies, dressed them for the grave,
poured out the last libation at the tomb.
Last, Polyneices knows the price I pay
for doing final service to his corpse.
And yet the wise will know my choice was right.
Had I had children or their father dead,
I'd let them moulder. I should not have chosen
in such a case to cross the state's decree.
What is the law that lies behind these words?
One husband gone, I might have found another,
or a child from a new man in first child's place,   910
but with my parents hid away in death,
no brother, ever, could spring up for me.
Such was the law by which I honored you.
But Creon thought the doing was a crime,
a dreadful daring, brother of my heart.
So now he takes and leads me out by force.
No marriage-bed, no marriage-song for me,
and since no wedding, so no child to rear.
I go, without a friend, struck down by fate,
live to the hollow chambers of the dead.   920
What divine justice have I disobeyed?
Why, in my misery, look to the gods for help?
Can I call any of them my ally?
I stand convicted of impiety,
the evidence my pious duty done.
Should the gods think that this is righteousness,
in suffering I'll see my error clear.

But if it is the others who are wrong
I wish them no greater punishment than mine.

Chorus
> The same tempest of mind
> as ever, controls the girl. 930

Creon
> Therefore her guards shall regret
> the slowness with which they move.

Antigone
> That word comes close to death.

Creon
> You are perfectly right in that.

Antigone
> O town of my fathers in Thebe's land,
> O gods of our house.
> I am led away at last.
> Look, leaders of Thebes, 940
> I am last of your royal line.
> Look what I suffer, at whose command,
> because I respected the right.

> (*Antigone is led away. The slow procession
> should begin during the preceding passage.*)

Chorus
Danaë suffered too.
She went from the light to the brass-built room,
chamber and tomb together. Like you, poor child,
she was of great descent, and more, she held and kept
the seed of the golden rain which was Zeus. 950
Fate has terrible power.

You cannot escape it by wealth or war.
No fort will keep it out, no ships outrun it.

Remember the angry king,
son of Dryas, who raged at the god and paid,
pent in a rock-walled prison. His bursting wrath
slowly went down. As the terror of madness went,
he learned of his frenzied attack on the god.   960
Fool, he had tried to stop
the dancing women possessed of god,
the fire of Dionysus, the songs and flutes.

Where the dark rocks divide
sea from sea in Thrace
is Salmydessus whose savage god   970
beheld the terrible blinding wounds
dealt to Phineus' sons by their father's wife.
Dark the eyes that looked to avenge their mother.
Sharp with her shuttle she struck, and blooded her
    hands.

Wasting they wept their fate,
settled when they were born   980
to Cleopatra, unhappy queen.
She was a princess too, of an ancient house,
reared in the cave of the wild north wind, her father.
Half a goddess but, child, she suffered like you.

                    (*Enter, from the side Teiresias, the blind prophet,*
                                   led by a boy attendant.)

Teiresias
    Elders of Thebes, we two have come one road,
    two of us looking through one pair of eyes.
    This is the way of walking for the blind.   990

222

Creon
  Teiresias, what news has brought you here?

Teiresias
  I'll tell you. You in turn must trust the prophet.

Creon
  I've always been attentive to your counsel.

Teiresias
  And therefore you have steered this city straight.

Creon
  So I can say how helpful you have been.

Teiresias
  But now you are balanced on a razor's edge.

Creon
  What is it? How I shudder at your words!

Teiresias
  You'll know, when you hear the signs that I have marked
  I sat where every bird of heaven comes   1000
  in my old place of augury, and heard
  bird-cries I'd never known. They screeched about
  goaded by madness, inarticulate.
  I marked that they were tearing one another
  with claws of murder. I could hear the wing-beats.
  I was afraid, so straight away I tried
  burnt sacrifice upon the flaming altar.
  No fire caught my offerings. Slimy ooze
  dripped on the ashes, smoked and sputtered there.
  Gall burst its bladder, vanished into vapor;   1010
  the fat dripped from the bones and would not burn.

These are the omens of the rites that failed,
as my boy here has told me. He's my guide
as I am guide to others.
Why has this sickness struck against the state?
Through your decision.
All of the altars of the town are choked
with leavings of the dogs and birds; their feast
was on that fated, fallen Polyneices.
So the gods will have no offering from us,
not prayer, nor flame of sacrifice. The birds   1020
will not cry out a sound I can distinguish,
gorged with the greasy blood of that dead man.
Think of these things, my son. All men may err
but error once committed, he's no fool
nor yet unfortunate, who gives up his stiffness
and cures the trouble he has fallen in.
Stubbornness and stupidity are twins.
Yield to the dead. Why goad him where he lies?
What use to kill the dead a second time?   1030
I speak for your own good. And I am right.
Learning from a wise counsellor is not pain
if what he speaks are profitable words.

Creon

Old man, you all, like bowmen at a mark,
have bent your bows at me. I've had my share
of seers. I've been an item in your accounts.
Make profit, trade in Lydian silver-gold,
pure gold of India; that's your chief desire.
But you will never cover up that corpse.
Not if the very eagles tear their food   1040
from him, and leave it at the throne of Zeus.
I wouldn't give him up for burial
in fear of that pollution. For I know
no mortal being can pollute the gods.
O old Teiresias, human beings fall;

the clever ones the furthest, when they plead
a shameful case so well in hope of profit.

Teiresias
Alas!
What man can tell me, has he thought at all . . .

Creon
What hackneyed saw is coming from your lips?

Teiresias
How better than all wealth is sound good counsel. 1050

Creon
And so is folly worse than anything.

Teiresias
And you're infected with that same disease.

Creon
I'm reluctant to be uncivil to a seer . . .

Teiresias
You're that already. You have said I lie.

Creon
Well, the whole crew of seers are money-mad.

Teiresias
And the whole tribe of tyrants grab at gain.

Creon
Do you realize you are talking to a king?

Teiresias
I know. Who helped you save this town you hold?

Creon
  You're a wise seer, but you love wickedness.

Teiresias
  You'll bring me to speak the unspeakable, very soon.   1060

Creon
  Well, speak it out. But do not speak for profit.

Teiresias
  No, there's no profit in my words for you.

Creon
  You'd better realise that you can't deliver
  my mind, if you should sell it, to the buyer.

Teiresias
  Know well, the sun will not have rolled its course
  many more days, before you come to give
  corpse for these corpses, child of your own loins.
  For you've confused the upper and lower worlds.
  You sent a life to settle in a tomb;
  you keep up here that which belongs below   1070
  the corpse unburied, robbed of its release.
  Not you, nor any god that rules on high
  can claim him now.
  You rob the nether gods of what is theirs.
  So the pursuing horrors lie in wait
  to track you down. The Furies sent by Hades
  and by all gods will even you with your victims.
  Now say that I am bribed! At no far time
  shall men and women wail within your house.
  And all the cities that you fought in war   1080
  whose sons had burial from wild beasts, or dogs,
  or birds that brought the stench of your great wrong
  back to each hearth, they move against you now.

226

A bowman, as you said, I send my shafts,
now you have moved me, straight. You'll feel the wound.
Boy, take me home now. Let him spend his rage
on younger men, and learn to calm his tongue,
and keep a better mind than now he does.   1090

(*Exit.*)

Chorus
Lord, he has gone. Terrible prophecies!
And since the time when I first grew grey hair
his sayings to the city have been true.

Creon
I also know this. And my mind is torn.
To yield is dreadful. But to stand against him.
Dreadful to strike my spirit to destruction.

Chorus
Now you must come to counsel, and take advice.

Creon
What must I do? Speak, and I shall obey.

Chorus
Go free the maiden from that rocky house.   1100
Bury the dead who lies in readiness.

Creon
This is your counsel? You would have me yield?

Chorus
Quick as you can. The gods move very fast
when they bring ruin on misguided men.

Creon
How hard, abandonment of my desire.
But I can fight necessity no more.

227

Chorus
Do it yourself. Leave it to no one else.

Creon
I'll go at once. Come, followers, to your work.
You that are here round up the other fellows.
Take axes with you, hurry to that place
that overlooks us.   1110
Now my decision has been overturned
shall I, who bound her, set her free myself.
I've come to fear it's best to hold the laws
of old tradition to the end of life.

(*Exit.*)

Chorus
God of the many names, Semele's golden child,
child of Olympian thunder, Italy's lord.
Lord of Eleusis, where all men come   1120
to mother Demeter's plain.
Bacchus, who dwell in Thebes,
by Ismenus' running water,
where wild Bacchic women are at home,
on the soil of the dragon seed.

Seen in the glaring flame, high on the double mount,
with the nymphs of Parnassus at play on the hill,
seen by Kastalia's flowing stream.   1130
You come from the ivied heights,
from green Euboea's shore.
In immortal words we cry
your name, lord, who watch the ways,
the many ways of Thebes.

This is your city, honored beyond the rest,
the town of your mother's miracle-death.

Now, as we wrestle our grim disease,   1140
come with healing step from Parnassus' slope
or over the moaning sea.

Leader in dance of the fire-pulsing stars,
overseer of the voices of night,
child of Zeus, be manifest,
with due companionship of Maenad maids   1150
whose cry is but your name.

(*Enter one of those who left with Creon,
as Messenger.*)

Messenger
   Neighbors of Cadmus, and Amphion's house,
there is no kind of state in human life
which I now dare to envy or to blame.
Luck sets it straight, and luck she overturns
the happy or unhappy day by day.
No prophecy can deal with men's affairs.   1160
Creon was envied once, as I believe,
for having saved this city from its foes
and having got full power in this land.
He steered it well. And he had noble sons.
Now everything is gone.
Yes, when a man has lost all happiness,
he's not alive. Call him a breathing corpse.
Be very rich at home. Live as a king.
But once your joy has gone, though these are left
they are smoke's shadow to lost happiness.   1170

Chorus
   What is the grief of princes that you bring?

Messenger
   They're dead. The living are responsible.

Chorus
Who died? Who did the murder? Tell us now.

Messenger
Haemon is gone. One of his kin drew blood.

Chorus
But whose arm struck? His father's or his own?

Messenger
He killed himself. His blood is on his father.

Chorus
Seer, all too true the prophecy you told!

Messenger
This is the state of things. Now make your plans.

(Enter, from the palace, Eurydice.)

Chorus
Eurydice is with us now, I see.   1180
Creon's poor wife. She may have come by chance.
She may have heard something about her son.

Eurydice
I heard your talk as I was coming out
to greet the goddess Pallas with my prayer.
And as I moved the bolts that held the door
I heard of my own sorrow.
I fell back fainting in my women's arms.
But say again just what the news you bring.   1190
I, whom you speak to, have known grief before.

Messenger
Dear lady, I was there, and I shall tell,
leaving out nothing of the true account.

230

Why should I make it soft for you with tales
to prove myself a liar? Truth is right.
I followed your husband to the plain's far edge,
where Polyneices' corpse was lying still
unpitied. The dogs had torn him all apart.   1200
We prayed the goddess of all journeyings,
and Pluto, that they turn their wrath to kindness,
we gave the final purifying bath,
then burned the poor remains on new-cut boughs,
and heaped a high mound of his native earth.
Then turned we to the maiden's rocky bed,
death's hollow marriage-chamber.
But, still far off, one of us heard a voice
in keen lament by that unblest abode.
He ran and told the master. As Creon came
he heard confusion crying. He groaned and spoke: 1210
"Am I a prophet now, and do I tread
the saddest of all roads I ever trod?
My son's voice crying! Servants, run up close,
stand by the tomb and look, push through the crevice
where we built the pile of rock, right to the entry.
Find out if that is Haemon's voice I hear
or if the gods are tricking me indeed."
We obeyed the order of our mournful master.
In the far corner of the tomb we saw   1220
her, hanging by the neck, caught in a noose
of her own linen veiling.
Haemon embraced her as she hung, and mourned
his bride's destruction, dead and gone below,
his father's actions, the unfated marriage.
When Creon saw him, he groaned terribly,
and went toward him, and called him with lament:
"What have you done, what plan have you caught up,
what sort of suffering is killing you?
Come out, my child, I do beseech you, come!"   1230
The boy looked at him with his angry eyes,

spat in his face and spoke no further word.
He drew his sword, but as his father ran,
he missed his aim. Then the unhappy boy,
in anger at himself, leant on the blade.
It entered, half its length, into his side.
While he was conscious he embraced the maiden,
holding her gently. Last, he gasped out blood,
red blood on her white cheek.
Corpse on a corpse he lies. He found his marriage.   1240
Its celebration in the halls of Hades.
So he has made it very clear to men
that to reject good counsel is a crime.

(*Eurydice returns to the house.*)

Chorus
  What do you make of this? The queen has gone
  in silence. We know nothing of her mind.

Messenger
  I wonder at her, too. But we can hope
  that she has gone to mourn her son within
  with her own women, not before the town.
  She knows discretion. She will do no wrong.   1250

Chorus
  I am not sure. This muteness may portend
  as great disaster as a loud lament.

Messenger
  I will go in and see if some deep plan
  hides in her heart's wild pain. You may be right.
  There can be heavy danger in mute grief.

(*The Messenger goes into the house.
Creon enters with his followers. They
are carrying Haemon's body on a bier.*)

232

Chorus
    But look, the king draws near.
    His own hand brings
    the witness of his crime,
    the doom he brought on himself.   1260

Creon
    O crimes of my wicked heart,
    harshness bringing death.
    You see the killer, you see the kin he killed.
    My planning was all unblest.
    Son, you have died too soon.
    Oh, you have gone away
    through my fault, not your own.

Chorus
    You have learned justice, though it comes too late.   1270

Creon
    Yes, I have learned in sorrow. It was a god who struck,
    who has weighted my head with disaster; he drove me to
        wild strange ways,
    his heavy heel on my joy.
    Oh sorrows, sorrows of men.

                *(Re-enter the Messenger, from
                a side door of the palace.)*

Messenger
    Master, you hold one sorrow in your hands
    but you have more, stored up inside the house.   1280

Creon
    What further suffering can come on me?

Messenger

Your wife has died. The dead man's mother in deed,
poor soul, her wounds are fresh.

Creon

Hades, harbor of all,
you have destroyed me now.
Terrible news to hear, horror the tale you tell.   1290
I was dead, and you kill me again.
Boy, did I hear you right?
Did you say the queen was dead,
slaughter on slaughter heaped?

      (*The central doors of the palace begin to open.*)

Chorus

Now you can see. Concealment is all over.

                (*The doors are open, and the
                corpse of Eurydice is revealed.*)

Creon

My second sorrow is here. Surely no fate remains
which can strike me again. Just now, I held my son in
    my arms.
And now I see her dead.
Woe for the mother and son.   1300

Messenger

There, by the altar, dying on the sword,
her eyes fell shut. She wept her older son
who died before, and this one. Last of all
she cursed you as the killer of her children.

Creon

I am mad with fear. Will no one strike
and kill me with cutting sword?
Sorrowful, soaked in sorrow to the bone!   1310

234

Messenger
  Yes, for she held you guilty in the death
  of him before you, and the elder dead.

Creon
  How did she die?

Messenger
                  Struck home at her own heart
  when she had heard of Haemon's suffering.

Creon
  This is my guilt, all mine. I killed you, I say it clear.
  Servants, take me away, out of the sight of men.   1320
  I who am nothing more than nothing now.

Chorus
  Your plan is good—if any good is left.
  Best to cut short our sorrow.

Creon
  Let me go, let me go. May death come quick,
  bringing my final day.   1330
  O let me never see tomorrow's dawn.

Chorus
  That is the future's. We must look to now.
  What will be is in other hands than ours.

Creon
  All my desire was in that prayer of mine.

Chorus
  Pray not again. No mortal can escape
  the doom prepared for him.

Creon

Take me away at once, the frantic man who killed   1340
my son, against my meaning. I cannot rest.
My life is warped past cure. My fate has struck me down.

(Creon and his Attendants enter the house.)

Chorus

Our happiness depends
on wisdom all the way.
The gods must have their due.
Great words by men of pride   1350
bring greater blows upon them.
So wisdom comes to the old.

A NOTE ON THE TEXT

The foregoing is a translation of the text of Jebb's third edition (Cambridge, 1900). In the dialogue, I have tried to bring into English almost all that I thought I saw in the Greek, even though this was to run the risk of a clumsy literalism. In the choruses, I have taken more freedom.

The following are the places where my rendering is of another text than Jebb's.

486 ὁμαιμονεστέρας A, other MSS, and the scholiast in L. ὁμαιμονεστέρα L, as corrected from –αις, Jebb.

The extravagance of imagining the impossible possibility of closer blood kin than a sister seems to me in character for Creon at this point. (For a similar use of language, cf. Aeschylus *Septem* 197.)

519 τούτους MSS and Jebb. ἴσους is recorded by L's scholiast and read by Pearson. Line 520 seems even more pointed if Creon is picking up Antigone's own term to throw at her.

572. This line is Ismene's in all the manuscripts. The only traditional evidence for giving it to Antigone is that the Aldine edition (1502) and Turnebus (1553) gave it to her. These editors may have had manuscript evidence lost to us. But they may also, like most modern editors, including Jebb, have been exercising their own sense of fitness. It is touching to have an Antigone stung from her silence to defend her lover. Further, if the line is not hers, we are faced with an Antigone who never mentions him; and much has been built on this.

The best argument for giving her the line is Creon's reply to it (573). If Ismene has 572 "your marriage" must mean

237

"the marriage you talk of," or words to that effect. This is possible, but the phrase would certainly come out more naturally to Antigone.

Confusions of speakers in stichomythia are many, and I see no possibility of certainty here. It is our misfortune that the line in question is an important one. I have stayed with the manuscripts, which seems to me all one can do.

574. This is Ismene's line in all MSS. Boeckh, followed by Jebb, gave it to the chorus. I have followed my own precedent in 572, and stayed with the MSS. The question might come, as Jebb argues, more reasonably from the chorus than from Ismene, who has had her answer already. But she is not too logical to ask the same appalling question twice.

600 κόνις MSS, Jebb. κοπίς Reiske and others, Jebb in earlier editions, Pearson. See Jebb's note and appendix. He was of two minds here. My own final feeling is that for dust to be doing the reaping is too much, even for a tragic chorus.

609 παντογήρως L, the MSS generally, L's scholiast. παντ'-ἀγρεύων, Jebb. This image was too strained for Jebb (and many others), as the dust in 600 was for me. De gustibus. . . .

904–20. Jebb (following and followed by many) brackets these lines, which are in all the MSS, and were known to Aristotle as Antigone's. I think he is wrong, but he should not be pilloried as a prudish Victorian for this. The positions of his note and appendix are well taken and held. Some sensible contemporaries (e.g., Fitts and Fitzgerald) are with him still. For those, like myself, who are sure the lines are Antigone's, there is drama in her abandoning her moralities and clinging to her irrational profundity of feeling for her lost and irreplaceable brother, devising legalistic arguments for her intellectual justification. Jebb finds the syntax of 909–12 strained past all bearing, but I believe Antigone's obscurity here is a touch of realism parallel to the confused and contradictory negatives of her opening lines, which Jebb allows her.

The Best of the World's Best Books
COMPLETE LIST OF TITLES IN
THE MODERN LIBRARY

A series of handsome, cloth-bound books, formerly available only in expensive editions.

MISCELLANEOUS

MODERN LIBRARY GIANTS

A series of sturdily bound and handsomely printed, full-sized library editions of books formerly available only in expensive sets. These volumes contain from 600 to 1,400 pages each.

THE MODERN LIBRARY GIANTS REPRESENT A
SELECTION OF THE WORLD'S GREATEST BOOKS